For my parents

Kamal Chandra Saikia

and

Lilawati Saikia

THE ASSAM MODEL OF DEVELOPMENT IN AMRIT KAAL

A development model for a
state that continues to
evolve and flourish
amidst the winds of change

KALPAJIT SAIKIA

ISBN

Paperback 979-8-89066-987-2
Hardcase 979-8-89133-730-5

TABLE OF CONTENTS

Chapter 1

PREFACE

During a short business trip to Tokyo, in 2018, one of my colleagues took me aside during lunch and asked for help. He said his son, in senior school, was doing a project on comparative analysis of some of the poorest regions of the world and wanted to include a few areas of India. He asked me if I could help his son with some information.

The next day, his son visited me at my hotel. He came with a questionnaire and wanted me to fill it up.

Looking at the questions, I told him, "It is not possible to know about all the states of India as it is a vast country, and my area of specialisation is also different."

He asked, "What states are you more knowledgeable about?"

"I have relatively better knowledge about two states. One is Karnataka, as it is the state I had been living in for around 20 years; the other is Assam, as it is the state where I was born, and I have a keen interest in its socio-economic aspects."

He looked up both states on his iPad and smiled. He said, "Karnataka may not be the right candidate for this research as it is more developed than the other states of India. But, Assam definitely fits the bill as it is one of the most underdeveloped Indian states."

I finished the discussion by providing him with some details about Assam. While I was not sure what parameters he used to analyse the relative development of both these states, it certainly changed something in me. It made me really think and rethink about the economic situation of the state of my birth. Probably, the factual analysis presented by a foreigner shattered my unconscious pride and led me to ponder over the sad economic state of affairs in my state. More importantly, it made me realise that despite living outside the state for a couple of decades and gaining exposure to extensive global perspectives on business and industries, I had done nothing to contribute to the development of the state I love the most in the world.

When I started doing research, I realised that the successive governments since independence had done nothing to industrialise the state. There may be legitimate reasons for their inability to do much in that direction because of constant strife and disturbances. But, the fact is that no effort was made in that direction, not even a futile one. Even the agricultural revolution, which made India self-reliant in a lot of areas, did not reach the state. There was no effort made to uplift the state industrially. In fact, one of the most industrialised states of India at the time of independence was reduced to a highly underdeveloped one by the end of the century.

But, what I found more disheartening was that there was no debate or discussion on businesses and industries in public forums. The media is quite silent in this aspect and the critics of industries have a field day in most of the public debates. Businessmen are the typical targets of most of these so-called intellectuals, and common people are made to believe that the main objective of the industries is to exploit them. As a result, any effort to promote industrialisation in the state is met with resistance, and there has been no significant effort to change that perception.

Then I saw a large number of people migrating from the state for low-level work. They work as security guards, delivery boys, and cleaning professionals across the country for a few thousand rupees of salaries. A complete lack of opportunities in their own state leads them to unknown territories where they try to make ends meet despite facing a highly challenging work environment. Assamese people were always reluctant migrants and were driven out only by unmanageable desperation.

To my horror, a minister of Industry, in one of the past governments, sent a team of officers to Bangalore to assess the employment potential for semi-skilled and unskilled people from Assam. The person who was supposed to promote industrialisation to create employment was looking for opportunities for the people of his own state in another state. It was unfathomable.

My generation has seen some of the most difficult times in Assam. We witnessed Assam agitation in our growing years, faced the dark days of insurgency of the late eighties and early nineties, and woke up daily to the news about ethnic conflicts.

While the reasons cited for those conflicts or agitations sounded logical, we knew that something was missing in those explanations. Much later, we realised that the foundation of those disturbances was not political or historical but rather economic.

The indigenous people were frustrated with their low living standards and lack of opportunities, while successful immigrant businessmen lived prosperous lives in their neighbourhoods. Similarly, the tribal population in parts of Assam experienced consistent underdevelopment and lack of job opportunities, while other communities got more privileges. These frustrations and anger were manifested in their effort to protect their land rights, language, ethnicity, customs, etc. Deep inside, everyone knew that if the economic situation had been better, none of these agitations would have taken place.

Things have changed since then. Most of the insurgent outfits were brought back to the mainstream or eliminated. The agitations have significantly reduced, and there is a focus on development. The government of India has introduced some landmark development programs in the northeast. The most ambitious among them is connecting the northeast to the Southeast Asian market. Infrastructure development is the key area of focus with the construction of roads, bridges, dams, etc. With the dynamic state and visionary central leadership, Assam seems to be pulling its socks and preparing for a long race of development. This gives much-needed hope to people like us who never saw good days while residing in the state.

In 2022, the prime minister unveiled the grand vision to make India a developed country by 2047. That made me think about Assam. What if India realises this vision? What if India becomes a 25 trillion dollars economy with a 10 thousand dollars per capita income? What if Assam is left behind in this growth story? What if Assam becomes a cheap supplier of labour to a highly developed economy? What if prosperity remains a distant dream for a highly deserving state like Assam? I understood that if Assam needs to be an equal partner in the growth story of India, the time to start is now. The Amrit Kaal for Assam should start now, and I decided to put my hat in the ring by writing my views on the ways to reach there. Doesn't matter how trivial, basic, unrealistic, or unimplementable my suggestions are, I am going to be one of the participants in the elusive debate on industrialisation of Assam.

About myself, I am not an economist or a social scientist. This book is not the result of any research program. The numbers mentioned in this book are mostly directional, and the views are personal. I am a corporate executive exposed to the dynamics of businesses across the globe. I do not claim that the solutions suggested in this book are perfect and ultimate. Also, the government must be implementing or has implemented a lot of these already. The government has extremely efficient machinery run by some of the most talented people in the country. There are good brains constantly working on various plans and programs for the development of the state. The intent of this book is to promote public discussion on making Assam a developed state by 2047, and while trying to meet that objective, if someone finds any suggestion outlined in this book implementable, it will serve more than its purpose. We all dream of a prosperous Assam, free from poverty, with a better standard of living, growth reaching every nook and corner, and of course, happy people.

I am a beneficiary of the development India has seen post-liberalisation. Hailing from a lower-middle-class family in remote Majuli with vernacular education, no one could have dreamt of scaling the difficult heights of the corporate world. I am not alone. There are thousands of successful professionals coming from average families with an average education who are becoming prosperous in the private sector across the world. We all have seen the benefits of an industrialised world, and now we want our compatriots to see it. I am sure, all of us dream of a day when all these jobs will be available in our home state, and no one will have to travel thousands of kilometres away from our motherland.

I am very unapologetic about my belief in my state and my people. I believe that Assam has the best potential to be a developed state. I also believe that the people of Assam are the smartest. These are not observations coming out of my emotional bias towards the state. With so many years in corporate, people build a fair amount of objectivity in their assessments. I think no Indian state has a better advantage than Assam for industrial development. Assamese people are not hardworking is an absolute myth. The fact is that Assamese people are not only hardworking but also extremely intelligent and can adapt to any environment. There is a strong fighting spirit that was utilised wrongly in different movements and agitations. If this spirit is channelled into entrepreneurship, there is no barrier that can stop us.

Though the tone and tenor of the book may sound like offering suggestions to the government, the targeted readers of this book are the common people. I have tried my best to keep the content simple and easy to understand as I want people, even those without a background in economy and business, to be able to read this book. People may read the book, analyse it, like it, dislike it, agree, disagree, argue, or write off. But, my only expectation is that people start a discussion on making Assam prosperous in the next 25 years.

I preferred to write it in English as I can type fast in the Queen's language and can complete the book quickly. Being a corporate executive, it's always difficult to find time to do anything outside the job, let alone write a book. I just took a quicker path. Though I am proficient in Assamese, my writing (typing) speed is dismal, and it would have taken years to complete the book. If people like this book, I would like to translate it into Assamese one day.

I am not a professional writer. This is my first book. There are bound to be errors. I will be indebted if these are pointed out and an opportunity for correction is given by the readers. As I said, the numbers are only directional. This is not a research book, so the numbers mentioned may have different reference years or origins. They are used for the analysis of a viewpoint only. There will also be repetitions of suggestions or points of view in many places to maintain the context of the discussion. A prolific writer may be able to avoid it, but a lack of experience in a rookie like me may compel the readers to go through the irritation of finding similar points on different pages of the book. Another apology for that.

I would like to thank my wife, Arnica, for giving me the confidence that I can pull off this stunt of writing a book. I am not sure whether there was any objectivity behind her confidence. My friend, Ravi K K has not only helped me put together the visual representation of the content in this book but has also been a pillar of strength throughout my short stint as a writer. From conceptualising the cover page to helping with the blurb, his imprint is everywhere in the book. He has been a constant influence in my life, and without his encouragement, writing the book would have always been a distant dream for me. Sudarshan Thakur, the secretary of Srimanta Shankardev Kalakshetra, is the reason I could finally pen my thoughts in the form of a book. I have never seen someone more convinced in the Assam story than him. It is because of him that I am still strongly and emotionally connected to Assam despite living almost a quarter century outside, and he makes sure this connection never breaks.

The success of this book will never be measured in terms of the copies sold. I will consider it a successful book if people discuss and debate the Assam model of development. It doesn't matter if the final development model is completely different from the suggestions I am offering in this book. What's important is that Assam should finally thrive.

Chapter 2

TRADE, BUSINESS, ECONOMY OF ASSAM: A HISTORICAL PERSPECTIVE

Like its political history, the economic history of Assam is also full of ups and downs. While it saw some glorious days of economic prosperity, there were also days of gloom and despair. The economic situation of any state is always linked to political stability, and Assam is no different. In the period of political stability, trade flourished, and strong economic growth was seen. However, there are also stories of exploitation and desperation of the common people in the long economic history of Assam.

In prehistoric times, temporary agriculture used to be a standard practice. There was a limited sense of property ownership in a place full of jungles and a very small population. Animal rearing was done mainly for consumption. In the later part of the pre-historic period, permanent settlements and cultivation was practised. In Mahabharat, Assam, then known as Pragjyotishpur, was a prosperous place with the availability of different types of valuable items like pearls, clothing, agar, gold, silver, etc.

During the reign of the Barman dynasty, there was some progress in the economy of the state. One of the most prominent aspects was the donation of cultivable land to Brahmins as a part of the 'Aryanisation' process. The king was the owner of all the land resources of the state. The people of the state were allowed to clear jungles and prepare the land for cultivation, but the king could acquire the land at any point in time. The peasants used to clear the land of jungles and make it ready for cultivation, and the king, in turn, used to acquire the land and donate it to the nobles and Brahmins. The peasants used to get a part of their produce for sustenance and hand over the rest to the owners. There used to be people with other professions like potters, ironsmiths, fishermen, etc. But, everybody used to do farming as those professions were not sufficient for their sustenance. Internal trade was very limited as the need was limited and everything the population needed was available locally.

As the currency was not in wide circulation, the ministers and other government officials were given land instead of salary. According to Huen-Tsang, the land was lowland but fertile, and there was good cultivation of paddy and fruits. The revenue for the treasury used to come from land revenue, trade income, import duty, tax on natural resources, tax from the rulers of occupied territories, fines from convicts, and proceeds from war. One-sixth of the produce was to be paid as tax by the farmers.

The settlements were largely self-sufficient and didn't need to depend on any external purchase. Once the settlements became permanent, production increased, and excess production started to be traded in a few markets. There was also the export of goods through the river route by the merchants. The boats used for the trade were owned by the King, and he and his officials were the traders; the profit from the trade was used to go to the exchequer. Gold, copper, silk clothing, rhino horn, and elephants' tusks were exported to various parts of India. Gold extraction by rivers like Subansiri and Dhansiri was a good source of revenue, and there were instances of export of gold to China also.

The Ahoms brought a strong culture of agriculture to Assam. When they arrived, Assam was inundated with massive land resources with limited cultivation. The permanent seasonal agriculture system was not widespread among the tribal population, and they used to change places each season for cultivation. Ahoms changed it.

Sihabuddin Talis, who came to Assam with Mirjumla, in his book *Fathiya-e-Ibriya* spoke a lot about the lifestyle and economic condition of the people. One important observation he made was about the large expanse of paddy fields touching the hills. There was a mention of the cultivation of various types of fruits apart from rice cultivation. There were around 10–12 thousand labourers employed to extract gold from the rivers. The extractors had to pay a tax of one *tola* gold to the king. The trades were conducted in gold and silver coins. There was no provision of land revenue, instead, the king was paid in the form of physical labour. There was literally no trade in the local markets, sometimes only betel nuts and paan were traded.

There was a lot of focus on development work by the Ahom kings. The roads, bridges, ponds, etc., were constructed by them. Ahom King Gadadhar Singha even started the process of organising land records.

During the rule of the Koch dynasty, there was an increased activity of trade with mainland India, Bengal, China, Tibet, etc. The government established a gate in Goalpara to manage the export of goods to other countries, and the official in charge of the gate, designated as *Duwariya Barua*, had fixed targets. There was export of cotton, mustard, silk, pepper, etc., and import of salt, pulses, spices, etc.

The *Tabakat-e-Nasiri* by Minhas-ud-din Chiraj mentioned about 35 mountain passes near Kamrup, Bengal, and Tibet for trade. There were many centres of trade close to the mountain passes through which trade and the exchange of goods used to happen. The trade extended even to Burma, China, Gujarat, and Kabul. The domestic trade was limited to betel nut, paan, domestic animals, and slaves. In the later part of the 18th century, local markets also came into existence and trade started taking place in currencies instead of a barter system. There were markets in places like Gargaon, Jorhat, Nazira, Titabor, etc.

One of the important aspects of Ahom rule was the 'Paik' system. Paik is the system of providing three months of physical service, yearly, to the state by the population of the age range of 16–50 years. In return, the state used to provide them with some land for cultivation without any tax. If someone wanted to opt out of the Paik system, they could pay some tax to the government and do it.

While the Paik system was prominent in Upper Assam, in the Kamrup area, people had to pay money as tax. There were fixed amounts for people with various professions. As per Sihabuddin Talis, the government used to earn around eighty thousand to one lakh rupees by extraction of gold from the rivers. There were other taxes like market tax, tax for crossing the river, tax on fishermen, etc. The assets used to be concentrated in the hands of a few government officials, priests, and the family of the king. It was a strange situation where common marginal people had to pay tax to the government in the form of money or physical labour, while the rich people were exempted from it. This came in the way of having a strong local economy. With the majority of the population being marginal, consumption was limited, and hence, local trade was almost non-existent.

The Burmese (*Maan*) invasion of Assam from 1817 to 1824 changed the social, economic, and political scene of Assam. Assam faced massive economic disaster during the invasion. There was indescribable loot and arson by the Burmese. Every person had to pay massive taxes. There was starvation everywhere. A lot of people fled to the hills of Garo, Bhutan, Cachar, etc. Burmese invasion broke the back of Assam's economy. The population was reduced to less than half. With Assam reeling under serious governance problems with the Moamoria revolt and the Burmese invasion, the arrival of the British was a sign of hope, and the population welcomed them with open arms.

Once, the British took the reins, they quickly realised that the revenue potential from their newly acquired territory was measly, and they started exploring other streams of revenue. Apart from the land revenue, one of the revenue sources identified was opium. In a span of 25 years, since 1826, the poppy output increased by three times.

In 1937, the British started their first tea Estate in Chabua, a small sleepy village in the eastern part of Assam. Assam Company was formed in the year 1939 and started commercial production of tea the very next year. The tea industry took off immediately. The tea output increased from around thirty thousand pounds on 2,311 acres in 1841 to more than ten lakh pounds on 8,000 acres in 1859. By 1860, 51 tea estates sprung up in various parts of Upper Assam.

With this increase in production came the problem of an acute shortage of manpower to work in the tea estates. The tea industry put huge pressure on the government to increase land revenue to discourage people from the cultivation of paddy and instead encourage them to become labourers in tea estates. It created massive economic hardship for the impoverished population. A lot of people surrendered their lands, and there were widespread protests. There was a huge disparity in tax collection from peasants and labourers of the tea estates. The tea estates also put pressure on the government to reduce the sale of opium, as there was widespread addiction that made it difficult to find labourers for the tea estates.

The government responded by banning poppy cultivation in 1860 because of which the price of North Indian Opium increased significantly. This further put huge economic stress on the population where a substantial number of people were addicts and needed their daily dose somehow. Despite all these measures, there was still a massive shortfall of labourers in the tea estates, so the planters tried to fill it by recruiting from the tribal regions of central India.

In 1874, Assam was separated from the administration of the Bengal presidency and reorganised into a separate governing unit under a Chief Commissioner. Brahmaputra Valley, Garo Hills and other hills districts, and Cachar initially constituted this new province to which Sylhet was added subsequently. This change was also triggered by the insistence of the tea lobby. Tea production increased manyfold in the new province. The production of tea increased from more than one crore pounds on 56,000 acres in 1872 to more than a hundred crore pounds on 3,38,000 acres in 1901. During the same time, capital investment in the sector increased by around 14 times.

There was an improvement in infrastructure with the construction of railways in 1881. Very quickly, the rail network expanded. From 114 miles in 1891, it increased to 715 miles by 1903. There was significant demand for coal by tea factories and railways. The coal output increased from 50 tonnes in 1871 to 2.77 lakh tonnes in 1905.

Economic activities intensified during British rule. Though it was for the self-serving reason of transporting their produce, the roads, bridges, and waterways were developed. Trading saw a major uplift, and the population increased at a faster pace. However, most of the beneficiaries of this development were the planters and upper-class businessmen; the local population was still on the margins. There was a serious imbalance between the traditional agriculture sector and new industries like tea, coal, oil, and associated trading. Though there was a net growth in terms of output in the economy, there was stagnation in food grain production due to which there was an increase in imports. The problem was accentuated by the emergence of the black fever epidemic (*kala jhar*), which wiped out a significant part of the population. On top of it, the exploitative British took out most of the gains from their businesses and taxes outside the state. There were also significant remittances of workers' wages sent outside Assam. The condition of the tea estate workers was even worse. The exploitative recruitment process, meagre wages, and slave-like treatment made their life even worse than that of the local population. In a nutshell, the only non-beneficiaries of the new industrial growth in Assam were the people of Assam.

Assam's economic journey post-independence is not even worth discussing. The reorganisation of the state continued till 1971, creating hindrances in the long-term planning and execution of economic policy. After Gopinath Bordoloi, there was always a dearth of strong visionary leaders. There was no serious effort to accelerate industrial activity in the state. Illegal immigration from East Pakistan and subsequently Bangladesh put a lot of stress on the already struggling economy. But, the factor that put a near-permanent break on Assam's industrial economy was the numerous agitations and extremism.

The per capita income of Assam in 1950–51 was 4% more than the national average. In 1998–99 it was 41% less than the national average. During the agitation and extremism-infested years from 1980–1998, Assam's per capita income increased by a mere 10%, while the growth for the country was 39%. Assam's economy grew at 3.3% compared to the national number of 6% between 1981–2000. The agriculture growth slumped from 2.1%

in the 1980s to 1.6% by the end of the 1990s. The industrial growth rate in the 1980s was a poultry 2.4%. From the beginning of the century, there have been marginal improvements in both the economy and industrial growth. But, the effects of political and social disturbances are still very much visible. Assam possibly will take a lot of time to recover from it.

There are improvements in the overall political situation now. The large-scale agitations are more or less contained, and the extremism has come to a complete halt. Successive governments post-2001 have tried to improve the economic situation of the state. There have been visible improvements. The GSDP has improved; the employment situation is better, and infrastructure developments are prioritised. But, in the area of industrial growth, there are still a lot of improvements required. There is a requirement for a strong push for setting up new industries and promoting entrepreneurship. In the subsequent chapters, we will explore various options and try to put forth some constructive suggestions.

Chapter 3

AMRIT KAAL AND ASSAM

It was on a hot Delhi morning of 15th August 2021, when the prime minister first mentioned the word 'Amrit Kaal' from the historic ramparts of the Red Fort. He defined Amrit Kaal as India's journey for the next 25 years to be a developed nation by 2047, the 100th year of India's independence. The nation is expected to aggressively and unitedly work towards achieving the objective of becoming prosperous. This is iconic and one of the most significant events in the short history of independent India. That speech and the subsequent pronouncements from the prime minister on Amrit Kaal is the most unprecedented expression of aspiration from a nation and the resolve of a billion people from one of the oldest civilisations of the world to reclaim its old glory. The prime minister said:

"There comes a time in the development journey of every country when the country redefines itself afresh and pushes forward with new resolutions. Today, that time has arrived in the development journey of India. We should not limit the occasion of 75 years of Indian independence to just one ceremony. We must lay the groundwork for new resolutions and move forward with them. Starting from here, the entire journey of the next 25 years, when we celebrate the centenary of Indian independence, marks the Amrit period of the creation of a new India. The fulfilment of our resolutions in this Amrit period will take us to the hundredth anniversary of Indian independence with pride."

The prime minister's focus so far had been in the area of the wholistic welfare of the citizens — the inclusion of all the citizens in the formal banking system, direct transfer of benefits to the beneficiaries, building basic amenities like toilets, providing clean cooking fuel to all households, and making the system accountable for inclusive development. On the industrial front, the focus has been on ease of doing business, attracting manufacturers to set up their base in India with make-in-India schemes, reducing export dependency by self-reliance, etc. But, this time, the vision is much larger. The prime minister further added:

"The goal of 'Amrit Kaal' is to ascend to new heights of prosperity for India and the citizens of India. The goal of 'Amrit Kaal' is to create an India where the level of facilities is not dividing the village and the city. The goal of 'Amrit Kaal' is to build an India where the government does not interfere unnecessarily in the lives of citizens. The goal of 'Amrit Kaal' is to build an India where there is a world-class modern infrastructure."

The prime minister recognised this is not a small task and will require a massive mobilisation of resources. Contribution from all the citizens will be needed to make this vision a reality. He further said:

"We should not be lesser than anyone. This is the resolve of the crores of countrymen. But the resolve remains incomplete until it is not accompanied by extreme hard work and courage. Therefore, we have to realise all our resolutions with hard work and courage. These dreams and resolutions are also for effective contributions to a safe and prosperous world beyond our borders.

'Amrit Kaal' is of 25 years. But, we don't have to wait for long to achieve our goals. We have to start now. We don't have a moment to lose. This is the right time. Our country has to change, and we, as citizens, have to change ourselves too. We also have to adapt ourselves to the changing era."

In the short history of the nation, India has seen many revolutions that helped the country become self-reliant and generated economic growth. Some of these are well publicised with larger impacts like the Green Revolution, which resulted in the self-sufficiency of food grain production, and the White Revolution, which made India the largest producer of milk and milk products and democratised the milk industry with the help of co-operatives. There were lesser-known missions like the Blue Revolution for fish production, the Yellow Revolution for oilseed production, and the Grey Revolution for fertiliser production. These helped the nation to inch towards self-sufficiency and economic progress.

Though successful, the impact of these campaigns was limited to specific areas and industries. Successive governments in the past have also implemented aggressive policies for industrial development, which created a strong growth momentum and lifted millions of people from below the poverty line. But, never in history, has there been a resolve for wholesome prosperity to propel the nation towards the goal of a developed country. Ten years ago, such a call would have been called absolutely outrageous. If successful, the story of the most populous nation with consistently low ratings on all the socio-economic parameters since independence becoming a developed country will be one of the most significant milestones in the history of mankind. That's why Amrit Kaal is expected to be the most extraordinary period in India's history.

The prime minister reiterated this mission in his Independence Day speech of 2022, and this time, he spoke about *Paanch Pran*, Five Resolves. Five Resolves to realise the dream of a strong and prosperous India by 2047 when the nation celebrates 100 years of independence. The first resolution is about making India a developed country. In his words, "Speaking of 'Paanch Pran', the first vow is for the country to move ahead with a big resolve. And that big resolution is of a developed India. Now we should not settle for anything less than that. Big Resolution."

What India has achieved in the last 75 years is not a mean feat. The British reduced India from a country contributing 23% to the world economy to a mere 4% when they left. Dependent on other countries even for food grains and basic necessities, the first 50 years of India's history was that of unending miseries and struggles. The prime minister knows that if a country with such a miserable economic condition can march to become the fifth largest economy in the world, the vision of India@100 is not unrealistic.

A few days after the famous speech by the prime minister on Paanch Pran and the vision for a developed India, the Economic Advisory Council to the Prime Minister and Institution for Competitiveness came out with a revolutionary paper, *Competitiveness Roadmap for India@100*. This roadmap has some elements that are unprecedented and revolutionary. It articulated other dimensions beyond GDP per capita to measure the prosperity of the nation.

India@100 proposed new guiding principles to achieve its goals. The GDP per capita is no longer considered a single benchmark of prosperity. Four additional dimensions are proposed to propel India to its vision.

- Prosperity growth needs to be matched by social progress.
- Prosperity needs to be shared across all parts and regions of India.
- Prosperity growth needs to be environmentally sustainable.
- Prosperity needs to be solid and resilient in the face of external shocks.

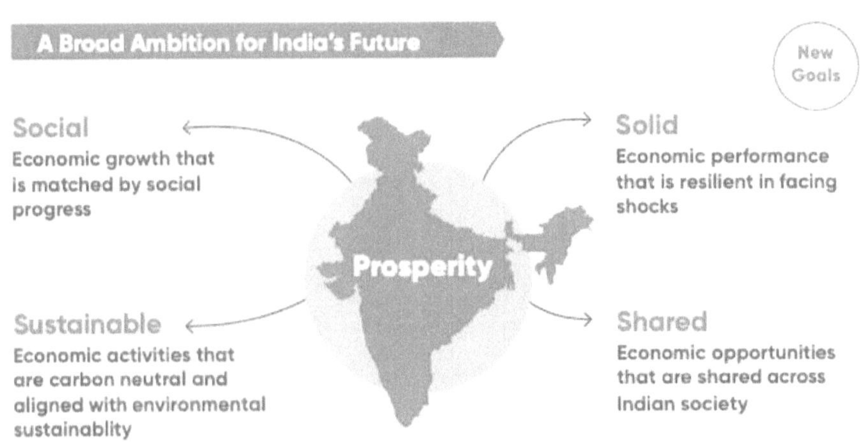

*Source: Competitiveness Roadmap for India@100 Report

According to the report, India's development agenda will be driven by two key principles. First is the integration of social and economic agendas. The core idea is to integrate both of these agendas creating competitive jobs for those currently outside the labour market. The objective is to move towards building highly productive and self-reliant individuals. Second is the structural transformation 2.0 to move beyond the traditional export-led industrialisation and adopt a portfolio-based approach for driving job creation across a number of service and industrial sectors.

These guiding principles are translated into focused policy action in India@100 strategy. Here is how the report explains the priorities for policy action:

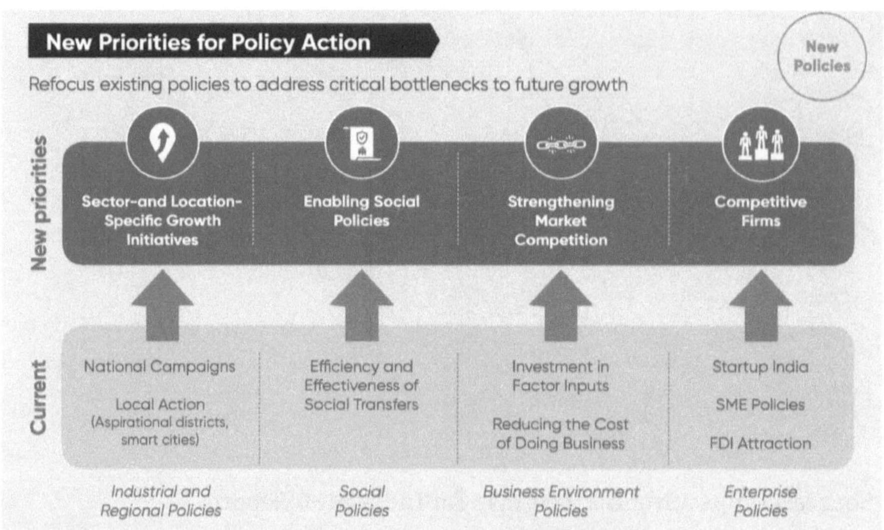

*Source: Competitiveness Roadmap for India@100 Report

"India needs to launch a new set of **sector- and location-specific growth** initiatives to reframe some of its key industrial and regional policies. Sector- and location-specific initiatives can identify the specific needs of individual clusters and regions and then select from generic policy tools to pursue a coherent strategy for growth and competitiveness upgrading. They will require tight collaboration between public and private sector leaders.

India needs to **enable social policies** that enhance the employability of labour market entrants and reduce barriers to getting a job. These policies will address urgent social needs across the country and trigger job creation opportunities. In some areas, that will require more resources, while in others, there is a need for regulatory change. Together, they exemplify the opportunities from complementary social and economic development, moving beyond the current welcome but insufficient focus on enhancing the efficiency of social programs.

Childhood poverty and the lack of accessible healthcare services can result in stunting and other developmental impediments that reduce children's productive capabilities throughout their lives. Low-quality education and the poor fit of available skills with the needs of the Indian economy create huge barriers to labour market entry. The provision of childcare services and investments in public safety are often critical factors for women to consider when looking for employment.

India needs to prioritise strengthening **effective market competition** as a central element of its efforts to upgrade business environment conditions. Deeply distorted market structures across many sectors are leading to poor outcomes, undermining the significant gains made in factor input conditions. Unfit regulatory frameworks and legacy market structures, reminiscent of different times, are holding India back.

India needs to adopt a comprehensive approach towards enabling the growth of **competitive firms**. It will require deploying a range of supply and demand policies and moving beyond current enterprise and industrial policies."

These are revolutionary ideas. For the first time in the nation's history, there is recognition that GDP is not the sole measurement of prosperity. If there is no balancing of economic prosperity with social and regional growth, it will not be sustainable, and competitiveness will be a distant dream.

India in Amrit Kaal clearly intends to move towards a solid growth path taking everyone across the country along.

There has been some work already underway in this direction. In the last few years, there have been sustained efforts to build a framework for an inclusive development paradigm. Be it direct benefit transfer, skill development, or *Jan Dhan Yojana*, the effort has always been to take the fruits of development to the lowest strata of society. With the current transformative initiatives, the intent is to make them an integral part of a prosperous India by increasing employability. This, coupled with the sector- and location-specific growth is expected to bring about a sustainable growth trajectory for the country. In terms of numbers, India targets to be a developed country by 2047 with a GDP of 25 trillion dollars and an upper middle-income country with a targeted per capita income of 10 thousand dollars.

Regional disparity is always a concern for India. In his election speeches, Prime Minister Narendra Modi highlighted this disparity with a vertical line in the middle of the country. While the western part of the country has prospered over the years, the eastern part is always struggling. Since then, there have been various efforts to bring some parity to the development objectives. Various infrastructure projects have been undertaken, efforts are taken to connect eastern India to a large market of southeast Asia, and river-based transportation is encouraged to fill the void of access to ports. Still, there are wide gaps. Even today, more than 50% of gross fixed capital formation happens in two large Indian states. The top seven states of the country contribute around 75% of merchandise exports. Almost 30% comes from one state in western India. The top five Indian states still contribute close to 50% of the country's GDP. On the face of these numbers, bringing regional economic parity is going to be a very tall task. In Amrit Kaal, this will definitely be a core area of focus.

The story of the northeast as a whole, and Assam in particular, is very different. Since independence, taking this region on the path of development was not an agenda item for Delhi. Its primary focus was controlling any dissidence arising out of historical and social reasons. There was no structured thought process, let alone an agenda to bring prosperity to the region with industrial development. The little development that Assam experienced was because of its rich natural resources and the revenue generated by the tea industry. While there were agitations and armed insurgencies, Delhi never understood that the core of the problems was regional disparity and poverty.

Things are changing now. The government rightly recognised that one of the biggest impediments to the development of the region is connectivity. There is a massive thrust given to improve connectivity both internally and externally. The India–Myanmar–Thailand trilateral highway and the Agartala–Akhaura railway link are considered to be two of the most strategic infrastructure projects undertaken by the country. There is a significant focus on internal connectivity also. Some states that were out of India's railway map for 70 years have been added to it and now all the states of the northeast have rail connectivity. Railways have undertaken 21 projects worth 95,261 crore rupees to build robust connectivity across all the northeastern states. The number of airports has doubled, and so has the number of flights. The number of airports has increased from 9 to 16 and the number of flights from 900 to 1600 in the last nine years. There is also a focus on digital connectivity with the fast laying of optical fibre networks.

There are visible results of these development initiatives. The agriculture product exports have increased by 85% and insurgency is down by 80%. The central government has removed AFSPA (Armed Forces Special Powers Act) from a majority of states in the northeast. This is a clear testimony that these disturbances were the result of years of neglect of the northeast by the ruling class in Delhi. The moment there were rays of hope for development, insurgency took a backseat.

Assam has seen some unprecedented growth in recent years. Its GDP is expected to grow at 15% and is targeted to reach 5.67 lakh crore rupees by 2023–24. There is robust growth in tax collection, and incomes from other sources have also increased. Welfare schemes like Arunodoi have helped in increasing rural consumption leading to strong inclusive growth.

For sustained economic development and mass job creation, the manufacturing sector needs to prosper. It is known that only manufacturing can bring inclusive development to a country. That's why India is targeting to increase the share of manufacturing in GDP from 17% to 25%. There are various programs and incentives to drive manufacturing growth. Assam also needs to put a lot of focus on this sector. Today, close to 70% of the state's population is engaged in agriculture, which contributes to 25% of the GDP. This is a huge mismatch. Unless the state can move more people from agriculture to manufacturing, prosperity will be a distant dream. In the next chapter, we will analyse why the emphasis on agriculture will be counterproductive to the economic growth aspiration of the state.

In Amrit Kaal, Indian states will face different kinds of challenges. The challenge of coping with the fast growth of the country. The states can either be strong contributors or laggards based on the policies and programs they execute. In a fast economic growth environment in a large country like India, some regions may fall behind and only work as a supplier of cheap manpower to the other rapidly developing regions. Take China as an example; China has been growing at an exponential rate for the last 40 years. But northeastern China was falling behind, while southern China was experiencing phenomenal growth. Today, southern China contributes around 65% of the country's GDP. At the same time, northeastern China was relegated to a poor region supplying cheap labour to the prosperous south. In a developed country like America, the per capita income of the state of New York is 100% higher than in Mississippi. The same is the story with a majority of the countries. It will be a complete failure of the endeavour of the nation if states like Assam fall behind the curve. In Amrit Kaal, Assam's quest will be to be a top contributor to the developed nation rather than falling behind and being dependent on the other prosperous states.

After Chief Minister Himanta Biswa Sharma took over, he expressed his intent to make Assam one of the top five states in the country. It will be a tough job when it comes to industrial development considering there is already a big gap with some of the highly industrialised states, but it is not entirely impossible. To achieve this, a different model of development should be envisaged that is not merely based on external investment.

The model needs to be innovative, aggressive, and different from the ones the states have adopted in the past. Assam needs its own model of development — The Assam Model of Development.

Chapter 4

ASSAM MODEL OF DEVELOPMENT

There is a development model behind every country's journey towards prosperity. The model comprises a combination of strategic, tactical, and operating plans to achieve the target goals. The goals are typically to increase GDP, per capita income, foreign exchange inflow, employment, etc. Bringing wholistic development for all the citizens is the dream of any developing nation. If we exclude countries that built their foundation of development through global hegemony and colonisation, the paths taken by most of the other countries are very interesting. These self-made countries took a methodical and well-planned approach, combined with commitment and dedication. One common factor that plays a key role in their development is the role of the government, which is extremely proactive and business-friendly.

The story of Germany and Japan's growth is fascinating. Though both were industrial powerhouses before World War II, they were devastated and had to start everything from scratch. Japan's model of development post-war was building an export-oriented industry, based on manufacturing and technology innovation. Likewise, Germany focused on innovation, engineering, and research and development. Their development model was to build world-class innovative products and establish itself as a global leader in engineering. While Japan's model was focused on volume-based manufacturing, Germany emphasised value. They became world leaders in their respective industries.

The stories of some of the Asian countries are equally fascinating. Singapore's story was about moving from a small and poor island to one of the most prosperous countries in the world. Their development model had a high focus on both trade and manufacturing. World-class infrastructure was set up in the form of airports, economic zones and ports, and attractive incentives were announced in the form of tax breaks and grants for the companies to set up their business in Singapore. Manufacturing was focused on high-tech and biotechnology areas. Singapore's march to a developed country happened in a very short time, and it is a big inspiration for any country aspiring for development.

Taiwan is another amazing story. Taiwan was an insignificant poor country when the nationalist fighters from China set up their base on this tiny island to escape the onslaught of communists. But, their resolve to march towards being a prosperous nation was unparalleled. They decided to be a high-tech and semiconductor manufacturing destination of the world. Large companies like Foxconn and TSMC (Taiwan Semiconductor Manufacturing Company) were formed and the entire ecosystem was built. Today, the country of 2.3 crore people is the fifth-largest economy in Asia and fifteenth largest in the world.

The development models of all these countries were conceptualised, planned, and executed by their highly committed governments. The government of Japan implemented strategies like the "priority production system" and "export promotion strategy" to fuel manufacturing and export growth. The essence of the famous "Japan Inc" model was to build a strong synergy between the government and businesses to collaborate, share resources and achieve the objective of industrial growth. The German government built their industrial development model by prioritising a few important areas. Firstly, they prioritised education and set up world-class applied research centres. They also funded vocational education and research institutes in the areas of science, technology, engineering, and mathematics (STEM). Secondly, they built a strong infrastructure to support industrial growth. Thirdly, they promoted SMEs very aggressively. These SMEs became industrial giants in the later years. The role of the Singapore and Taiwan governments was even more hands-on. Leaders from these countries travelled around the world to convince business leaders to invest in their countries. They went to the extent of preparing the outside-in business case to persuade the investors. There is this famous story of the Taiwanese prime minister making several trips to America to convince the legendary Morris Chang to come to Taiwan and help set up a semiconductor industry. The government eventually convinced Mr Chang to head the Industrial Research Institute before helping him set up TSMC with a capital contribution of a hundred million dollars.

Back home, we have the story of the Gujarat Model of Development led by the then Chief Minister Narendra Modi. Gujarat model comprised a combination of industrial development programs in the form of Special Economic Zones and tailor-made incentives to invest in the state while focusing on the other key aspects of growth in the rural areas with programs related to agriculture. These, combined with effective welfare schemes, helped the state move towards prosperity. The famous story of the message to the Tata Group Chairman, Ratan Tata, inviting him to set up his factory in Gujarat at a time when he had to relinquish his plan to start his operations in West Bengal due to land acquisition problems talks volumes about the government's active role in the industrialisation process.

Why do we need a separate Assam model? Is the model of development adopted by the government of India not good enough? To get an answer to these questions, let us first understand how much Assam needs to scale to become a strong contributor to India as a developed country by 2047. Currently, Assam's GDP is around 60 billion dollars, and it contributes around 2% to India's GDP. Back-of-the-envelope calculation says that Assam needs to grow at a rate of around 8% till 2047 to maintain the same percentage of contribution to the projected Indian economy of 25 trillion dollars. Assam's Chief Minister has articulated his vision of making Assam one of the top five economies of the country. That will require a consistent growth of around 14% (considering the current share of 7.87%

contributed by the fifth largest state in terms of GDP). These are large numbers, and there are only a few instances of such consistent growth over a period of 25 years in any economy.

Assam also has some inherent limitations. Unlike its counterparts, Gujarat and Andhra Pradesh, which have an abundance of arid lands and can be converted to industrial zones with a system of water supply, Assam has no such advantage. Assam also has the limitation of not having a seaport, which can facilitate the smooth movement of goods. Though the insurgency and agitations have reduced significantly, there is still a sense of discomfort for the investors to whole-heartedly put their hard-earned money into a business in the state. Frankly, when it comes to choosing between a state like Gujarat or Maharashtra and Assam, the choice is abundantly in favour of the former. Assam needs a different development model if it wants to achieve its vision of becoming an economic powerhouse.

Let us address another important question. Why industries and why not agriculture? Assam is traditionally an agrarian state blessed naturally with a good climate and riverine system. Can it not build a vision for prosperity around agriculture?

The answer to this question lies in the fundamentals of agriculture. Agriculture is always constrained by capacity. This means, unlike manufacturing or services where the production output can be increased manifold by the addition of new factories or manpower, there is no such scope in agriculture where land volume is going to be the same. A farmer can increase his income only by increasing yield or cropping intelligently. The output will still be limited. In Assam, the problem is even more acute. Being an inheritor of fertile land

and friendly weather, it has been inhabited by a large number of people dependent on agriculture. Close to 70% of the population is employed in agriculture, out of which 80% are small and marginal. Agriculture is not a lucrative profession anymore. Farm sizes are decreasing rapidly and the number of marginal farmers is increasing. The cost of production is often higher than the selling price. A study conducted by the Centre for the Study of Developing Societies (CSDS) in 2018 revealed some alarming facts. The survey conducted in 18 states found 76% of farmers preferring to move out of agriculture and 61% of them wanting to move to cities, while 62% of the farmers didn't even know about Minimum Support Price (MSP). The situation will be far worse if the government doesn't work at lightning speed to arrange alternate professions for the farmers.

Targeting prosperity on the face of these numbers is impossible. Compare these to the world's largest agriculture producers. World's largest agricultural producer, China employs around 24% of their labour force in agriculture. That number for Ukraine, one of the largest producers of wheat, is around 14%. Despite being the largest exporter of agriculture, the USA employs less than 2% labour force in agriculture. Automation has taken over the majority of their farming work. Back home, in Punjab, one of the largest producers of agriculture, only 26% of its population is engaged in farming.

There is clearly an imbalance. Assam employs much more people in agriculture than it should. The main reason for it is not the profitability of the trade, but the lack of other avenues. A 25% contribution to GSDP with the employment of 70% population is not healthy for any economy and can have a catastrophic effect on the economic condition of the population.

Ramesh Chand, a member of Niti Aayog, in one of his papers titled *Transforming Agriculture for Challenges of the 21st Century* clearly said, "During the 25 years after 1991, the share of agriculture in the workforce declined to around half in Brazil, China, and Malaysia. The labour share of agriculture in Vietnam declined by about 40 per cent. In the case of India, the decline has been much smaller (one-third). This has created serious structural imbalances between the sectoral composition of output and employment."

The immediate focus of the government is to pull more people out of agriculture to other sectors. That's why it is important to focus on intelligent cropping and yield improvement, but encouraging more people to take up farming will be a damaging proposition, and it will take Assam behind in its economic growth story.

Assam can have its own priorities for policy action that are aligned with the national action plan. These priorities will be the foundation for policymaking and the creation of operating plans for the next few years. These can change based on the progress in a particular area or alteration of ground reality. Some of the key considerations while defining these policy priorities can be as follows:

Considering the task at hand and the current realities, the priorities need to be **aggressive, replicable, and inclusive**, which can drive visible outcomes in a defined period. There can be time-bound goals and objectives defined against each priority area that can be reviewed on a regular basis. Replicability is extremely important as any success in a particular area should be replicable in other areas or other states within the country. Assam can be a role model and impart knowledge, being in line with the great traditions of the country. The priorities can be designed in such a way that benefits the larger population from every stratum of society rather than a select few. These priorities can drive visible outcomes within a specified period of time. In any public policy execution, unless there is a visible outcome, the feeling of scepticism creeps in, and the initiative is considered to be ineffective. These outcomes need to be widely publicised to maintain the confidence of the people.

The second consideration for defining these policies is that they should have a **combination of both immediate and transformational goals**. The march for a prosperous Assam needs to start immediately as time is precious, but there can also be space for some large transformational initiatives that will result in taking this growth to an exponential level.

Technology should be considered an integral part of efficient governance. In today's world, no organisation can work efficiently without the effective adoption of new-age technologies. The aspiration of prosperity for Assam will also bring a fair amount of competition with other states and countries. To be ahead of the curve, we will require technology, not only as an enabler but as an inherent part of any decision-making by the government. While setting the priorities, the state should provide immense emphasis on **technology as a means to empower governance.**

One of the very noticeable aspects of any policy action in recent years in India is that its effect on life and livelihood is always considered. The same can be the case when Assam formulates its priorities. The priorities should have a **strong impact on the life and livelihood** of the people of the state.

Lastly, these should be in **alignment with the national vision**. India@100 report provides an unconventional roadmap for the country towards prosperity. Assam's priorities should align completely with it. No state will be able to independently achieve its objective of economic prosperity without the active support and collaboration of the central government. The central government should also be a key stakeholder in the state government's initiatives.

Assam's Priorities

There are four priorities Assam needs to work on to accomplish its vision of a developed state. These encompass the key areas of inclusive industrial development while focusing on efficiency, transparency, and quick execution.

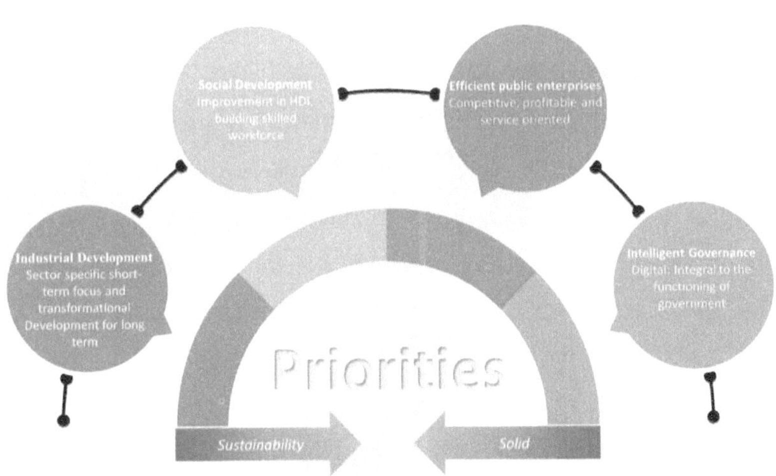

One of the most important priorities for policy action in India@100 report is sector- and location-specific growth. Assam's model of **industrial development** can have space for the promotion of resilient and scalable local enterprises as well as attracting investments from established businesses. There can also be a vision for transformational growth that can provide steeper growth momentum. The combination of both will form the foundation of the Assam Model of Industrial Development and form the most important pillar of priority for the Assam government in Amrit Kaal.

Historically, industrialisation in Assam was limited to the oil and tea industry in which the intent of industrialisation was more for the exploitation of natural resources and unique geographical advantage by the British. Post-independence, there was no strategy for the industrialisation of the state, and hence, it remained mostly an agriculture-based economy. Social disturbances also didn't help in bringing investments to Assam. Because of the exploitative nature of the industries set up in the past, the people of Assam have always been very suspicious of any industrial activity. Entrepreneurship was not prevalent, and the local population preferred to opt for a safe government job rather than setting up a business. Things are changing. There are investments in natural resources industries or in sectors where businesses can take advantage of the government's incentives. A lot of businesses are set up in Assam to cater to the increasing demand from both Assam and other consuming states of the northeast. But, there should be guaranteed long-term sustainable industrial growth for the state. Today, Assam is growing at a higher rate than the national growth rate. But, if a strong campaign for an industrialised state is not undertaken, it will not last long. There is a need to build a sustainable and resilient vision for Assam's industrial growth.

Massive infrastructure initiatives by the government of India in the northeast will bring Assam in close proximity to large Southeast Asia markets. India itself is growing, and consumption will increase manifold. Large export markets are opening up due to changes in geo-political alignments to reduce dependency on China by various countries. While India has been a strong global player in the knowledge economy, and that thrust will continue, the government is emphasising increasing merchandise exports significantly. This is the most ideal environment for any state to build a vision for industrial growth.

On the **social development** front, enhancement of employability in the labour market and improving the rating in the Human Development Index can be the key priorities. Emphasis on technical and vocational training can help enhance employability. Early interest identification and skill development linked to industry requirements can be a focus area. On the HDI front, a lot needs to be done to get Assam to the top contributing states in the country. The early identification of risk areas and taking steps to mitigate them quickly can be key to success. Accountable governance at the grassroots level and intervention of technology can be the approach to make an impact on social and economic progress.

Efficient government enterprises are core to any economic development mission. Government enterprises are the foundation of building a prosperous state, and making them efficient must be a key priority. To aid the development process, the service delivery from these enterprises will be very critical. Inefficient services will be a big roadblock in the process. Also, government resources will be very precious during the process of industrial growth. Spending it to run inefficient enterprises will create a significant bottleneck in this effort. The approach to building high-performing government corporations can range from changing business models to introducing innovative practices and technology intervention. It is important that instead of consuming the government's resources these enterprises work as role models for emerging businesses, set an example of strong governance, and provide the much-needed service delivery to a booming industrial environment.

And lastly, there is no alternative in today's world apart from going digital and running an **intelligent government**. This is a very important pillar of the government's priorities. Intelligent government encompasses all the aspects of governance and social issues. The governance should go beyond traditional digitisation and citizen services. There can be an increased emphasis on the use of technology to build a strong real-time decision support system and predictive models. Intelligent governance also means integrated governance. There should be a single version of the truth and no silos when it comes to governance. There can be an endeavour to have truly intelligent governance using digital technologies.

These four pillars can form the basis for setting policies and building execution plans for Assam's prosperity. In the next few chapters, we will elaborate more on each of these pillars.

Chapter 5

INDUSTRIAL DEVELOPMENT

There have always been debates on the approach a state should take for Industrial Development. Different models are suggested by experts based on the ground realities and constraints. No model is perfect. There is always scope for improvement and the possibility of accommodating other ideas. The objective of this chapter is to provide a point of view that can be further deliberated and refined. The ground reality of Assam is that it is not an advanced industrial economy, and there is a transformational push required to match the targeted growth of the country by 2047. At the same time, there is a requirement to build the right industrial environment for such transformational initiatives. Hence, Assam's endeavour for exponential industrial growth can have two streams:

- Industry sector and entrepreneurial development as a near-term focus

- Aspirational and iconic growth for the long term through transformational initiatives.

Industrial Development – Two-pronged approach

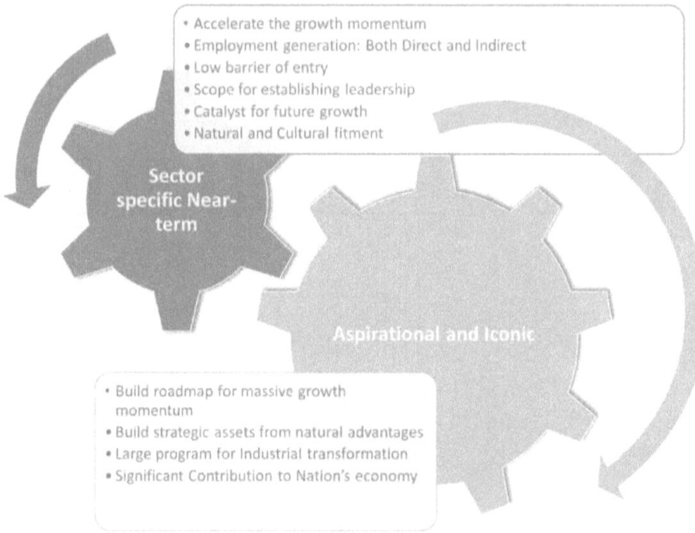

Near-term growth through industry and entrepreneurial development can be achieved through a focus on both domestic and export markets. Indian domestic market is very large. In an approximately 3.75 trillion-dollar Indian economy, currently around 23% is contributed by exports. Even if this number increases to 40% by 2047, in a 25 trillion-dollar economy, the GDP from the domestic market will be 15 trillion dollars, which is just a little less than the current GDP of China. Fulfilling the requirements of a 15 trillion-dollar economy requires a massive manufacturing ecosystem. Merely by addressing the domestic market itself, Assam can have a flourishing economy. With no trade barrier, geo-political uncertainty, duty impact and risk of loss from volatile currency markets, the domestic market can be a catalyst in Assam's growth story.

There is also a large export market to be explored. If there is a 40% share of exports in the economy by 2047, the total size of India's export is expected to be 10 trillion dollars. Assam can take it as a mission to contribute at least 5% of that number. No mean task considering the total exports by India in the year 2022–23 is only around 775 billion dollars in which 450 billion dollars is total goods exports. The fundamental of developing the export market is to achieve the required scale and quality. That will require investment from established players. While the established strategy is to provide world-class infrastructure, attractive incentives, and special benefits for anchor companies, Assam can also explore options to promote industries that align with the inherent strength of the state. The generic approach of exploring the wider market for exports may not be very effective as the barrier of entry is high, and the cost of promoting the business may outweigh the immediate benefit expected from it.

While working on initiatives that can get results in the near term, transformational opportunities can also be explored. Going back to the numbers, achieving more than 13–14% consistent growth for 25 years will require support from large transformational initiatives. It is important that the natural advantages of the state should be leveraged to build a framework for transformational initiatives. While the goal of such initiatives is to have exponential economic growth, there can be plans for stagewise realisation of the benefits. It goes without saying that such initiatives will require large investments, partnerships with multiple stakeholders, and massive mobilisation of resources. This cannot be accomplished by the state government solely and will require extensive support from the private sector and the central government.

Near-Term Focus

There has been a significant change in the way the top economic powers of the world are running their trade with China in recent years. For more than three decades, global manufacturers have been relocating their manufacturing to China purely for cost advantage. China has also supported them, year after year, by forcefully keeping the labour cost low and manipulating the currency markets. This was a mutually beneficial arrangement till China started using its economic might to assert itself as a global power both politically and militarily. The United States and other Western countries became increasingly concerned with China's growing power and realised that the only way to control it was to weaken its economy, and the best way to do so was by reducing import dependency on China.

Most of the major economies of the world run a massive amount of trade deficit with China. America, the largest trading partner of China, runs a trade deficit of around 382 billion dollars. Similarly, the EU's trade deficit has increased significantly after the pandemic, almost touching 400 billion dollars. But, these numbers are expected to decline in the coming years. The trade deficit with the US reduced in 2019 and 2020 before marginally increasing in the next 2 years. There is a clear understanding that it is not possible to reduce the trade deficit with coercive means in the globalised economy. The only way to do it is to move manufacturing out of China, and the process has already started.

Companies have also realised that in an uncertain political environment, it is best to look for alternate manufacturing destinations outside of China. Business disruption because of the "Zero Covid" policy of China also made them realise that it is best to de-risk by expanding their manufacturing footprint to other countries. India, being a stable democracy with a strong demographic advantage is one of the top contenders when it comes to alternate sourcing locations. In recent months, there have been some good investments from the high-tech and semiconductor industries. It is expected that this will extend to other industries also. Though it is not possible to replace China completely as a global manufacturing capital, there will be increasing focus by global companies to de-risk their sourcing, and India will emerge as the right alternative.

India itself is trying to improve its trade balance by trying to be self-reliant. India's total merchandise trade deficit in 2022 was around 266 billion dollars of which 85 billion dollars was with China. The government's focus in the next few years will be to reduce this trade deficit significantly. It will provide massive opportunities for Indian businesses. The strategy of *Atmanirbhar Bharat* with aggressive PLI (Production-Linked Incentives) and capital subsidies will pay good dividends in the coming years.

India's domestic market is quite large. India's FMCG sector has grown from 31.6 billion dollars in 2011 to 110 billion dollars in 2021–22 and is expected to reach 220 billion dollars by 2025. India has become the third-largest automotive market in the world in 2021 with a volume of 22.93 million vehicles. The total revenue generated by the industry is more than 100 billion dollars. Around 45 million jobs are created by this industry. Indian Appliance and Consumer Electronics (ACE) market reached 69.15 billion dollars in 2023 and is expected to grow at 5.89% CAGR. The FDI has almost doubled from 2021 to 2022 in the sector. The overall electronics market size currently is 140 billion dollars with 62% domestic production. Domestic production is expected to reach 300 billion dollars by 2026. Domestic electronics production has doubled from 2017 to 2022, and there is 5X growth in domestic mobile production from 2015–2023. The capital goods industry is expected to reach 112 billion dollars by 2025. The white goods industry has done 13.66 billion dollars and is expected to reach 21 billion dollars by 2025. The turnover of the pharmaceutical industry was 42.34 billion dollars in 2021–22 and 23.5 billion dollars of that was revenue from exports. The textile industry is expected to reach 250 billion dollars by 2025. These numbers are quite staggering, and a large industrial economy can thrive by only targeting a market as large as India. That explains the reason why global companies are flocking to the Indian market and trying to get a share of its pie.

With the prospect of global businesses shifting their base and bustling domestic demand, India is on the cusp of massive economic growth. Assam needs to pick up speed and try to grab the advantages. It will be understandably difficult to attract global businesses to set up their manufacturing base in Assam immediately because of the issues related to the industrial environment and infrastructure. But, in the near term, the mammoth Indian market is up for grabs for Assamese businesses.

The government can promote industries that generate large-scale employment with less capital investment, it can also look at the industries that can be growth engines for the future. It can initially focus on a few industries, try to make them successful, and then look to expand the list. In this chapter, we will discuss six such industries.

Apparel: Revenue from India's textile and apparel industry was estimated at around 100 billion dollars in 2023, employing 45 million people and expected to grow at 12% CAGR. A labour-intensive industry with low capital investment, this can be the industry that can change the face of the unemployment situation in Assam.

Plastic Goods: A fast-growing industry dominated mainly by MSME. There are close to 30,000 plastic processing units in India today. With the government's clear focus on decreasing imports from China, this industry will grow very fast in the next few years. There will also be a strong domestic demand as per capita plastic consumption in India is still very low compared to other economies and is expected to increase significantly in the next few years.

Meat: India has the largest population of livestock and is the largest producer of buffalo meat and the second largest producer of goat meat. But, the most widely consumed meat in the world is pork. The current market size of pork is 254 billion dollars, which is expected to reach 418 billion dollars by 2028. With the right planning backed by scientific farming, the pork industry can take Assam's economy to newer heights.

Tourism: Though a lot of actions have been taken in this sector in Assam in recent times, there is scope for more. Assam has the kind of natural advantages that very few states in India can match, and it's time to convert these advantages into an industrial boom. Tourism has the ability to change the face of a country's economy, and its impact can reach a large part of the population through both direct and indirect employment.

Pharmaceutical: India is a global leader in the generic pharmaceutical industry, and it is expected to see exponential growth in the next few decades. The pharmaceutical industry not only generates employment but also helps bring much-needed forex to the country. It is a high-margin business, which means that there can be a better standard of living for people employed both directly and indirectly. The functioning of pharmaceutical manufacturing requires the support of a lot of ancillary units. There are instances where the entire economy of a large area is positively impacted by a pharma manufacturing unit. This can surely be a future growth engine for Assam.

Medical devices: With a total market size of more than 400 billion dollars, the medical device industry has seen significant growth in the last few years. While there is advancement in this sector with innovative technologies by established players, this industry is also seeing a significant transformation from an institution-focused industry to one focusing on end consumers. With the advent of standardised manufacturing practices, there is also an increase in outsourcing. Currently, India imports close to 80% of its medical devices, putting further pressure on its trade deficit, which is increasing year on year. India's medical devices import increased by 41% in 2021–22 compared to 2020–21. The government of India is putting a lot of effort into reducing this import dependency and will be at the top of its agenda on self-reliance.

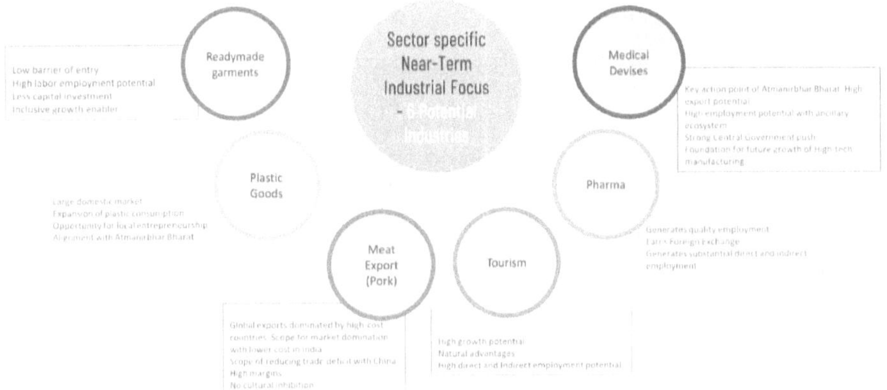

Business dynamics are changing everywhere. New destinations are emerging as industrial hubs and traditional locations are facing challenges. A fast-developing country requires multiple industrial hubs to balance its growth. Assam can be one of those emerging industrial hubs of India. Let us analyse each of these industries one by one. It is important to mention that this list can expand or change based on more extensive studies or the emergence of new ideas.

Apparel Industry

The best way to start industrial activity in a state with high unemployment and a poor track record of a friendly industrial environment is to target a labour-intensive industry with low capital investment. The low capital investment reduces the risk associated with setting up the industry, and if skilled manpower is available at a lower cost, the industry finds it an attractive proposition to invest in. Apparel is one of the industries that fit the profile.

With a global market size of approximately 1.5 trillion dollars, apparel is one of the largest generators of employment across the globe. The revenue from this industry in India is estimated at around 100 billion dollars, employing nearly 45 million people, more than the total population of Assam. This industry contributes approximately 2% of the country's GDP and 12% of the overall export earnings. There is also good FDI investment in this sector.

The domestic market in India itself is quite large. The readymade garments market size is around 40 billion dollars; the ethnic wear market and the kids wear market are 10 and 17 billion dollars, respectively. A small share in the domestic market itself will be several billion dollars.

The topmost driver for investment in garment manufacturing is the availability of skilled manpower at low cost. Historically, this industry moved from Western countries to low-cost destinations like China and India. Subsequently, the industry explored other destinations like Sri Lanka, Indonesia, Bangladesh, Madagascar, etc.

In India, Mumbai, Delhi, Surat, Ahmedabad, Tirupur, and Bangalore are traditional garment manufacturing destinations. Each of these locations specialises in a particular type of apparel. While Bangalore specialises in high-grade readymade menswear, Delhi is famous for denim and ladies' western wear. Surat is the destination for ladies' ethnic wear, and Tirupur is known for knitwear. Other small towns are also picking up as manufacturing hubs mainly because of their cost advantage and availability of manufacturing know-how. Jabalpur, Kanpur, Indore, etc., are slowly becoming attractive destinations for domestic apparel.

The apparel industry helps improve the standard of living of the lower-income groups drastically. One country that has seen phenomenal growth in apparel manufacturing, particularly ready-made garments, is Bangladesh. Readymade garment exports in Bangladesh have grown from 14.6 billion dollars in 2011 to 42 billion dollars in 2021–22. The industry employs a workforce of approximately 4 million, largely comprising poor and marginalised people. As women constitute the majority of the workforce, the improvement in living standards had a larger impact on the overall socio-economic indicators. The family sizes in Bangladesh have fallen drastically from 6 in 1980 to 2 today. The average life expectancy has increased by around 20 years since the 1980s. The ratio of women to men's manpower also has increased from 26 in 1990 to around 45 today. Though there are a few isolated instances of poor living standards for garment workers, the truth is that there is an overall improvement in their lives and livelihood. This kind of prosperity can be clearly seen in places like Bangalore where the total household income of garment workers is often more than that of mid-level government employees.

Garment manufacturing is highly cost-sensitive. A slight increase in per-piece manufacturing cost impacts the profitability of an entire unit. The industry is highly dependent on a skilled workforce and the scope of automation is very low. Manufacturers look for alternate destinations if traditional manufacturing locations become unviable because of an increase in labour costs. Assam can try to build itself as the next destination for garment manufacturing. There is a large women population ready for employment in the state who can be equipped with the required skills. The relatively lower cost of living in the state can also ensure that wage levels can be kept low and cost-competitiveness can be ensured. Assam can formulate a comprehensive policy and take important executive actions to start developing the industry in the State.

Apparel manufacturing is a broad area categorised into multiple sub-areas. Based on fabric quality, they are divided into woven, knitted, and polyester garments. Based on end-use, there are different types of garments like men's readymade garments, ethnic wear, suits, sarees, etc. The operational aspects like sourcing and manufacturing defers for different apparel types and hence, the strategy for the promotion of the industry can be devised at a sub-category level.

Till the time the industry matures and can have its own demand-supply dynamics, the government must play a larger role, and it can start from the identification of the segment it intends to promote. Targeting specific industry segments within apparel will provide a much-needed focus, help build specialised skillsets, and help make targeted policy decisions. The best industry to start with is woven Readymade Garments (RMG). This industry has large domestic and export markets, has standard production processes, and can provide employment to a large number of people. Access to raw materials is relatively easy, and it is less polluting compared to other segments. However, this industry is highly competitive, and the government will have to work on strategies to help the manufacturers build efficiency and keep the cost of operations low.

Once the industry segment is selected, there is a need to identify the challenges of setting up the business and formulate effective policies to address these. For example, in a landlocked and remote state like Assam, transportation will always be a challenge. As the nearest raw material sourcing location and port are thousands of miles away, the government will have to offer adequate transport incentives. Similarly, there is a set-up time needed for a manufacturing unit till it reaches its target capacity levels. This set-up time will be longer for a new manufacturing location as there is less possibility of recruiting an experienced workforce who can deliver results quickly. Hence, the government may need to announce incentives that will compensate industries for lesser productivity in the initial set-up time. There is also a need for incentives for supporting industries like washing and packaging units. These incentives will help industries find a favourable cost-benefit driver for setting up manufacturing units in the state.

The apparel industry is run by skilled labour, and very often, the availability of cheap and skilled labour becomes the primary decision point for setting up a plant in a specific location. Development of a pool of skilled labour force should be done in close coordination with the industry. Unless it is done with a firm commitment from the industry, these trained resources will become migrant labourers in other established manufacturing locations. The strategy of getting the required assurance from the industries to set up their units and skilling the workforce accordingly requires a combination of sound planning, tailored policy support, and a strong and convincing business case.

The right infrastructure is the key for any industry to survive. Apparel parks with good infrastructure with 24-hour electricity and water supply are basic requirements. The locations of these parks should be chosen intelligently. If it is very far from the main cities, it will be a logistical nightmare. If they are very close to the city, the high cost of living will lead to high wages making the unit practically unviable for manufacturing activity. The facilities can be customised for the target industry to the maximum possible extent. For example, the structure of the building to accommodate a woven readymade garments production line will be different from that of ethnic wear. Customised infrastructure can reduce the set-up time of a new factory.

Apparel manufacturing is not a high-margin business, and even a small disruption can have a large impact on the profitability of the business. Assam is infested with terrible domestic disturbances for most of its time post-independence. Agitations, protests, and insurgencies always managed to repel the investors. Though the situation has been more or less normalised in recent years, businesses will still be very wary of investing in the state when they have better alternative destinations. The government can work out a business continuity guarantee scheme, which will include financial compensation in case of business disruption because of any external factors like agitation, lockdown, strikes, etc.

Care for the environment should be an integral part of any industrial promotion strategy. Some operations of the apparel industry are highly polluting. The washing units require the usage of large quantities of polluting chemicals, and if not disposed of or recycled properly, they can create a massive health hazard for the population. Some states paid the price for not focusing on this aspect while setting up the industrial areas. A few years back, the garment industry in Tirupur had to literally shut down to conform to pollution control norms. Had the government envisioned the same at the time of setting up the industrial area, this could have been avoided. The government of Assam can devise norms for the protection of the environment and share clear guidelines with the industries.

There is also a possibility of exploitation of workers in a highly labour-intensive industry. As the industry grows, numerous small job work units may mushroom, employing a large labour force. While large industrial houses may have structured labour policies, there is a possibility of exploitation in the smaller job work units. The government should work out strong yet non-disruptive policies to avoid exploitation of the workforce and an effective grievance redressal mechanism should be devised.

The apparel industry can change the employment scenario of Assam and the biggest beneficiary of this industry will always be the poor and marginalised people.

Entrepreneurship Revolution with Plastic Goods

Plastic is one of the most widely used materials in the world. The current market size of plastic products is estimated at around 580 billion dollars and is expected to be 750 billion dollars by 2028. The growth of plastic is significantly increasing in the automotive, construction and electronics sectors. In automotive, the constant pressure of reducing the weight of the vehicles to attain fuel efficiency is leading to the substitution of metal parts with plastics. Similarly, there has been a spurt of construction activity after the pandemic and the industry is expected to double its size in 10 years from 2020 to 2030. Despite the pandemic, the electronics industry has grown by around 6% leading to high demand for plastics in the industry. In India, plastic consumption is led by the packaging industry with 43% share followed by infrastructure with 21% and automotive with 16%.

The interesting aspect of the plastic industry in India is the domination of small and mid-sized units. Around 85–90% of the total 30 thousand processing units in the country are small and mid-sized units employing around 40 lakh people.

The domestic market is also very promising. India's per capita plastic consumption is around 15 kgs, lower than the world average of 28 kgs and far below the per capita consumption of other prominent economies. America's per capita consumption is 139 kgs, and the number for China is 46 kgs. Despite this low per capita consumption, India is the third largest consumer of plastics contributing 6.4% of the total global use. There is going to be a significant increase in plastic consumption in the years to come. The total demand for plastic products is estimated to increase from 15 million tonnes in 2021–22 to 160 million tonnes by 2060.

India's plastic production is also going to increase significantly in the years to come. The 'Atmanirbhar Bharat' campaign is expected to intensify plastic production in India. India imported 19.15 billion dollars' worth of plastic products (including raw materials) in the April–January period of 2022–23. This number is expected to go down drastically, and Indian manufacturers will try to bridge the demand-supply gap.

Here again, the state needs to take the approach of promoting an industry segment rather than the entire industry. The segmentation needs to be based on the type of finished product. To identify the focused category of the finished product, criteria like high market demand, easy accessibility to raw materials, low entry barrier, simple manufacturing process, quick set-up time, etc., need to be considered. The growth of the industry will be driven predominantly by small and medium businesses. Plastic toys, commercial packaging products, or home utility products can be some of the segments to consider. Manufacturing for automotive OEMs or the medical device industry will need specialised expertise and higher quality standards. Hence, there can be a plan for attracting investment in these segments from established players. Special skills are required for some segments of the industry and professionals should be roped in to help build and execute strategies.

As the industry will be dominated by small and medium businesses, financial support can be the foundation of policy formulation. Capital subsidies, working capital support, incentives in the areas of power, and finished goods transportation need to be considered in the initial period of building the industry. For the segment of manufacturing specialised products, additional production-linked incentives will attract the industries to invest in the state.

Training entrepreneurs and skilling the workforce will be important. For entrepreneurs, an understanding of the market, manufacturing processes, financial management, and workforce management are very important. The government can enable new entrepreneurs and make them ready to run their businesses as quickly as possible. We will discuss more about the extent of support the government can provide to the industries in the subsequent chapters.

Considering the nature of the business, it is important to allow the establishment of manufacturing units only in the designated economic zones. The industry can be highly polluting; allowing the manufacturing units anywhere in the state will lead to the government losing control over environmental priorities. Also, there may be interdependency of different manufacturing units and efficiency will be far better if they are within the same geographical vicinity. The marketing, sourcing, and sharing of resources will also be convenient if these industries are in the same area. Hence, setting up plastic industrial parks can be a priority.

The industry will require support in marketing, sourcing, manufacturing know-how, and quality control for the initial period. Till the industry attains maturity, achieves cost competitiveness, brings out innovative and high-quality products, and becomes well-known in the market as a reliable source of goods, it will require strong marketing support. The government can form a marketing agency to dedicatedly promote the products manufactured by the units. For the initial few years, this unit can be the sales and marketing arm of the new enterprises. The marketing unit will identify potential buyers, connect them to the manufacturers and help accomplish successful transactions.

The small and medium units will not achieve a cost advantage in sourcing if they source individually in small quantities. There will also be quality concerns about the sourced raw materials. The credit terms will also not favour these units. The government can support them in many ways, like providing information on credible raw material sources, identifying quality details, consolidating requirements from different units for better commercial terms, etc.

It is extremely important to look into the quality control aspect. It may not be possible for the new units to have a complete understanding of the quality management process. The government can have a quality control task force within the industrial parks to help the units with the right processes and train them on maintaining consistent quality standards.

While the promotion of the industry is very important for the economy, it should not be done at the cost of the environment. The plastic industry can be a source of major pollution and if not controlled properly it can bring disaster to the environment. Hence, it is important to have a strong and stringent policy for pollution control. The manufacturing units should be allowed to be set up only in designated industrial parks. The parks should have a strong waste recycling/disposal system. Strong air pollution control systems and equipment should be installed and operationalised. There should be proper checks to ensure any form of pollution is under complete control. The entire mission will fail if we cannot control the environmental impact of the industry efficiently.

The promotion of plastic goods manufacturing can create a local entrepreneurship revolution, and Assam is best placed to start it.

Pork Meat Industry

Meat is one of the largest industries with around 900-billion-dollar global revenue in 2021. It is expected to grow to 1.3 trillion dollars by 2027. Meat consumption is increasing with rapid urbanisation and high disposable income. This industry is a major source of foreign exchange for many countries, and if promoted well, it has the potential to be the primary driver of economic prosperity for Assam.

India is the fifth largest meat producer in the world with an annual production of 9.29 million tonnes for the year 2021–22 and growing at an annual rate of 5.62%. With the world's largest livestock population, India accounts for around 3% of the world's meat production. Maharashtra and Uttar Pradesh are the leaders in this industry followed by West Bengal and Andhra Pradesh. India exports more than 4 billion dollars' worth of meat every year. The domestic market in India is also booming and is slated to grow at a faster pace in the next few decades. India's per capita meat consumption is still around one-eighth of the global number. This number will increase manifold giving a much-needed boost to the industry.

Assam has a unique advantage when it comes to the meat industry. With almost the entire population non-vegetarian, there is no major cultural barrier for the industry. Except for the religious aspect of the prohibition of certain types of meat, the acceptance level for meat in the state is fairly high. Pork meat is widely consumed in most parts of Assam, and it is becoming one of the preferred meat options for the local population. Hence, for a majority of the population, rearing of this animal is not a taboo unlike in the other parts of the country.

The economic potential of pork meat is huge. Pork meat is the most consumed meat in the world comprising around 35–40% of the global consumption. The global pork market was valued at 254 billion dollars in 2022 and is expected to grow at a rate of 8.6% and reach 418 billion dollars by 2028. Some countries have immensely benefited from pork exports. Pork export amounts to around 2% of the total export of Spain. The United States' export of pork meat to China was so important in their trade relationship that it was one of the agenda items in the trade talks between both countries. Japan, which imports more than 4.5 billion dollars' worth of pork meat every year has to be dependent on high-cost products from US and Canada. The potential in this industry is huge. China has the unique distinction of being the largest producer, consumer and importer of pork. The top global merchandise exporter needs to import pork meat to meet its domestic demand, and that's a great area of opportunity for countries like India, which is trying to reduce its trade deficit with the red dragon.

There are three key elements that determine the success of the industry. Breeding, quality control, and animal feeding. The most important among them is the pig breed to be bred. Multiple characteristics make a breed desirable to be bred. Product quality, carcass yield, fast growth, lean-gain efficiency, meat flavour, and cleanliness are some of them. To devise a strategy to promote the industry, it is important to understand the target markets to be served and the kind of pork meat required there. There is a lot of preparatory work and research required to identify the target markets and determine the kind of pigs to be bred to address the needs of these markets.

The identified breed can be imported and reared in a controlled environment under stringent quality standards. Upon successful breeding, the piglets can be made available to the selected entrepreneurs trained sufficiently to handle all aspects of pig rearing in line with global standards. Initially, farming should be allowed only in designated farms in which farmers can be allocated sites. This will help the government agencies to have better control over aspects like rearing standards, feed quality, growth, etc. Each identified area can have a government-run breeding facility for the identified type of pigs from which the pig farmers can source it. These are important steps in the initial stage of promotion of the industry as the farmers will be unaware of the kind of animal required and the skills to breed and rear it. The process can be handed over to the farmers or independent businesses once the industry matures. In each step of the process, close collaboration with the Pig Research Institute will be required. In fact, the government can take advantage of the knowledge base, resources, and facilities available at the institute in the initial period.

The most important aspect of the meat industry is the emphasis on quality. Meat imports are highly controlled by the respective governments, and they demand the highest standards of quality. There are prescribed norms by each country's food safety departments. The import is never allowed unless those norms are fulfilled. Despite having flourishing industries, there are instances of failed inspections leading to massive losses for the farmers. Right guidelines and training on the quality standards and processes need to be imparted to the entrepreneurs. A quality control team can be attached to the pig farms to constantly monitor and provide the right recommendations to the businesses to meet the quality standards.

Feeds play a significant role in pig farming. The quality of the meat is directly impacted by the quality of animal feed, and hence, the development of the animal feed industry should be an integral part of the pig industry's development. A similar approach of incentivising, marketing, and manufacturing support needs to be taken.

The government can encourage local entrepreneurship in this industry. The right know-how and quality control training can be provided to entrepreneurs. A facility of decent size is required to achieve the economy of scale and also to attract external buyers. The government can promote cooperative farming in designated areas to build the scale.

The most important aspect of the promotion is marketing support. The entrepreneurs will not have the required muscle power to access the lucrative markets and attract buyers. The government can take the role of active facilitator in providing marketing support. Existing trade agreements can be taken advantage of, and there can be independent agreements with large importers. The central government's support will be very critical for the success of the industry.

Last but not least, there should be an emphasis on sustainable farming. There are issues like deforestation because of the deliberate destruction of forest cover to make space for the animal ranching and feed industry in top meat-producing countries. There are also allegations of massive water usage in the meat production and processing industry leading to scarcity of water in the vicinity of the industry. There are also issues like diseases transmitted through animals and increased risk of spread to other species. There can also be a possible imbalance between traditional agriculture and animal farming leading to scarcity of food products and inflation.

The government should be aware of possible threats to the environment and take preventive steps to avoid them. It should formulate strong policies to ensure these threats are mitigated even before the industry is promoted. There should be strict laws to prevent the industry from adversely impacting the environment. There should be a limit to the number of production and processing units in a particular location. The government can also have a mechanism to detect the onset of a disease in animals and take concrete steps to contain it. The African swine fever was almost like to blow to the pork industry in recent years. Efforts should be taken to localise a disease/virus and not allow it to be transmitted to the entire industry. The bottom line is, no industry can sustain if it causes an adverse impact to the environment. It is in the interest of both mankind and the industry to ensure all the environmental norms are adhered to.

The meat industry can contribute to Assam's economy immensely. With the right strategy and efficient execution, this industry can bring life to the overall industrial scenario in Assam.

Tourism Industry

No other state in India can claim to have better natural advantages than Assam in tourism. A rare combination of long beautiful valleys on both sides of the mighty Brahmaputra, charming unexplored hills, places of historical ruins, many locations of mystery, and four distinct seasons. These are all the catalytic ingredients of a tourist destination. Tourists, both domestic and international, visit Assam in large numbers. Still, not even a fraction of the enormous tourism potential of the state is explored yet and the number of tourist footfalls can be much more than what it currently is. The good news is that the scenario is changing fast and there has been aggressive action from the government in the last few years to promote this industry.

Pre-pandemic, the global tourism industry was worth around 10 trillion dollars contributing almost 10% of the global GDP. One out of every five new employment was generated by the travel and tourism industry between 2014 to 2019. According to the World Travel and Tourism Council (WTTC), despite the slump created by the pandemic, the industry bounced back to contribute 7.6% to global GDP and created 22 million new jobs in 2022. Domestic tourist spending increased by 20.4% and international tourist spending by 81.9% in 2022 from 2021.

The Indian tourism industry is booming currently and the future outlook is also very bright. Despite the effect of the pandemic, there was a footfall of 677 million people in 2021 in the country. In the same year, the tourism sector created 12.91% of the total jobs in the country. In the year 2022, the arrival of 6.19 million foreign tourists was recorded. This sector is expected to contribute 250 billion dollars to the nation's GDP and generate 137 million jobs and 56 billion dollars in foreign exchange earnings by 2030.

The scenario in Assam is also quite encouraging. The granting of industry status to the sector is increasing private investment. Several government incentive programs including capital subsidies are rolled out. The promotional campaigns are also quite effective. There is a conscious effort to promote new destinations beyond Guwahati and Kaziranga. The results are also visible in tourist arrivals. In 2022–23, Assam crossed the magical number of one crore tourist arrivals, which is a jump of more than 500% from the previous year.

But, there is still a lot of scope for improvement. Though an important milestone, the arrival of one crore tourists is still less than 1.5% of the total domestic visitors. This number can go up manifold. The foreign tourist arrival numbers are small but significant. Around 20,000 foreign tourists visited Assam in 2022–23.

In the past, Assam's performance in tourism was dismal. Numerous agitations and extremist activities broke the back of the sector for a long time. The governments also didn't take any initiative to improve the situation. Till the beginning of the century, there was literally no activity. Apart from traditional tourist attractions like Kaziranga, where there have been good tourist movements mainly because of it being a "World Heritage Site" and the enthusiasm of some of the local entrepreneurs and businesses, the overall tourism scenario was disappointing.

Proper tourist infrastructure was also lacking. With no private investment, Assam Tourism Development Corporation (ATDC) built a few properties in prominent tourist locations. But, in the absence of proper management, the condition of these properties deteriorated over time.

Tourism is the industry that has the ability to positively impact a larger population across various spectrums of society. From big businesses owning luxury resorts and transport companies to small-time traders or hawkers, everyone can benefit from progress in this sector. In a true sense, this sector can bring inclusive development and can create direct and indirect employment opportunities.

Governments have recognised the immense capability of the industry to transform lives and are investing a good deal of resources in it. Not every state is naturally destined to have so many tourist attractions like Assam. There are examples of completely unconventional locations transforming themselves into lucrative tourism destinations. For Assam, it is all about employing the right strategies, taking required policy decisions, and going ahead aggressively to promote the industry.

To understand the kind of strategy Assam needs to employ, let us first look at a couple of success stories in India. One of the first states to realise the importance of the industry and take aggressive steps to promote it is Kerala. Kerala has the natural advantage of having some exotic destinations and an extremely supportive government. In fact, Kerala was the first state to designate tourism as an industry. Kerala's tourism brand 'Kerala: God's Own Country' is incredibly popular and considered to be one of the iconic branding exercises in India. Today, tourism contributes around 10% to the state's GDP and more than 20% to employment. But still, in 2019, Kerala was 7th in India's international tourist destinations and didn't even feature in the top 10 domestic tourist destinations.

On the other hand, Gujarat is not bestowed with a lot of tourist attractions traditionally. Apart from Gir National Park, Somnath temple, Sabarmati Ashram and a few other sanctuaries, Gujarat had nothing much to promote when it came to tourism. Weather is also not very conducive for a great tourism experience. When it started its mega campaign, *Khushbu Gujarat Ki*, no one could predict the kind of success it would get. The baritone voice of Amitabh Bachchan requesting people to visit Gujarat with the tagline — *Kuchh din toh gujariye Gujarat mein* — was also not expected to get the tourists to make a beeline for this naturally disadvantaged state. But, 11 years down the line, Gujarat has become one of the fastest-growing tourist destinations. In 2019, it ranked 9th in domestic tourist destinations and 12th in international tourist destinations.

There is a lot of learning from both these models. Kerala's tourism strategy was based on a model promoted, backed, and invested in by the government. The government developed a huge accommodation infrastructure and promoted them heavily. The Kerala government's tourism expenditure is massive. In 2019, it was around 1.27% of the total state expenditure, while the national average was around 0.49%. The tourism department in Kerala implements its infrastructure projects through various agencies and PSUs. Though the State's Vision 2025 document clearly emphasised the participation of the private sector with the state acting as a facilitator, the government's role is still significantly high in infrastructure development. There is a conscious strategy to promote Kerala as a boutique tourism destination attracting high-spending tourists. In a massive country like India, one cannot ignore the enormous revenue generated by domestic tourists. In summary, though tourism in Kerala saw good successes with heavy government involvement and niche positioning, it is proven to be not a sustainable model.

On the contrary, the Gujarat model is purely based on private investments. It can be very clearly seen in the tourism policy of 2021–25. While the government is a facilitator and involved in strategic infrastructure investment, attractive incentives are provided to the private sector for investing in tourism. The success of some of the unconventional tourist destinations like Rann of Kutch can be attributed to the private sector. Globally, this model is the most successful and scalable, and the state of Assam can also have a strategy based on private sector participation.

Two main pillars of tourism development are Promotion and Infrastructure. The standard process is to identify the tourist circuits and exclusive destinations for the target customer segment and promote it with the right advertising and media plan. A circuit is developed around a traditional tourist favourite or combining a few. A domestic tourist requires at least two or three destinations to be combined to have a meaningful tourism experience. For example, in Assam places like Kaziranga, Majuli, and Sivasagar can be promoted as one circuit for a weeklong experience. The storyboards are developed by experts to simulate the experience on paper. Once it is accepted, the required development plan is made.

The necessary infrastructure can be built with the help of the private sector. Adequate incentives can be provided to the private sector to invest in accommodation and other recreational infrastructure. An attractive capital subsidy is the key to developing tourist infrastructure. But, all these incentives are provided by every state of India, and hence, it is important to understand the compelling reasons for the investors to invest in Assam than other successful tourist locations. Investors need a quick return on their investment and that can be achieved only when their investments are protected. In tourism, the best way to go about it is by providing exclusivity to a destination or project for a period that justifies the investment. With that, the businesses can plan their promotion and development without any fear of competition snatching their revenue.

This is easier said than done considering the intense public scrutiny on such arrangements in Assam. The local population should be made key stakeholder in the projects, and they can be the advocate of such commercial arrangements. To excel in tourism, Assam needs to move beyond the old ways and build integrated resorts, world-class spas, themed attractions, museums, etc. In an emerging tourist destination, these cannot be done without such an arrangement with the private sector.

The ideal way to go about it is to form statutory corporations under the tourism ministry to manage the affairs of a tourist destination. The corporation can form various companies with private investments to run specific development programs at a destination. With this approach, it will have independent governance and accountability and be able to perform without any interference. Like any for-profit organisation, the companies will work on a blueprint and roadmap for the development of a specific location, build a robust business plan, arrange the required funding, and run the business. There should be learning from other corporations like Sentosa Development Corporation of Singapore.

The government's role as facilitator and regulator is very important. There can be district-level tourism promotion councils to monitor the state of tourism in the district. Skill development is another focus area. Lack of quality manpower can take the sheen off the industry. The availability of qualified tourist guides, hospitality staff, chefs, etc., is very critical to the success of the industry. There can be training programs to develop the industry-ready workforce. Enough awareness and training can be provided to the people, in general, to deal with the tourists.

There are cultural nuances involved when it comes to a tourist destination and enough care should be taken to adapt the local population to the flow of tourists. The objective of treating tourists well and addressing any untoward incident should be a key focus of the district tourism promotion councils. It must be noted that a small incident can spoil the name of a destination and have a direct impact on tourism for many years. The government should also focus on the safety and security of the tourists. Law enforcement agencies should be agile and sensitive to the needs of tourists. Special care is needed to take care of the environment in the tourist destinations. There should be enough manpower to ensure the cleanliness of the tourist locations, and proper guidelines should be provided to the tourists to prevent any damage to the environment.

Another successful segment of tourism is medical tourism, and India is emerging as one of the top medical tourism destinations. With its high-quality medical facilities at low cost, it is the ideal destination for most of the neighbouring countries, which lack advanced medical facilities. In 2022, around 1.4 million medical tourists visited India. Assam has the advantage of being in close geographic proximity to countries that rely on India for advanced medical care. Bangladesh comprises around 50% of medical tourists to India, and Assam can target taking a major share of that with the advantage of distance and cultural similarities. The trilateral highway will open a lot of opportunities for medical tourism with visitors from other Southeast Asian countries.

Anyone who travels to Assam falls in love with the scenic beauty, weather, and hospitality of its people. This can be by far the best tourist destination in the country and can contribute massively to the economy of the state.

Pharmaceutical Industry

The pharmaceutical industry is one of the most successful industries in India. The Indian pharmaceutical industry is ranked 3rd globally, in terms of volume, and 14th in value. It addresses 60% of the global demand for vaccines and almost 40% of the generic products in the largest pharmaceutical market, the USA. With around 3,000 pharmaceutical companies and more than 10,000 pharmaceutical manufacturing units, India's total export of pharmaceutical products reached 23.5 billion dollars, contributing to a trade surplus of around 15 billion dollars in 2021–22. India accounts for 20% of the global generics business with around 60,000 generic brands in 60 therapeutic categories. The domestic market is also flourishing. According to the Economic Survey 2021, the domestic market is expected to grow three times in the current decade. Currently, the industry is estimated at 42.34 billion dollars, which will further expand to 130 billion dollars in the year 2030.

Assam is cognizant of the immense benefit this industry brings to the economy and has taken multiple steps to promote it in the state. The establishment of Biotech Park in Guwahati, Pharma Hub in Balipara, and Pharmaceutical Park in Chaygaon are steps in the right direction. In recent times, several Indian pharmaceutical companies have also started their manufacturing units in the state. Though these are positive developments, there is scope for more considering the immense growth potential of this industry.

Based on the type of drugs manufactured, pharmaceutical companies are broadly divided into two types—Proprietary and Generic. Proprietary Pharma companies are the ones who come out with a new drug, which is a new cure for a disease or a better option for an existing drug available in the market. This requires extensive research and clinical trials, spanning multiple years (sometimes decades) and necessitating massive investments. There is always a possibility that after many years of research and millions of dollars of investment, a drug may fail, and all the investment may go down the drain. As a reward for the innovation, a new drug developed by the proprietary companies is given a patent for a specified period. During this time, the company has an exclusive right to sell the drug to reap the benefit of its innovation and get a return on its investment. Global pharmaceutical giants like Pfizer, Novartis, and Merck are proprietary pharmaceutical companies.

The drug patents expire after the specified time is over, and once it does, any company with the capability to manufacture the drug can go ahead and produce it. That's when the role of generic players comes in. The generic manufacturers pick up the drug formula, manufacture it, and make it available to the general population at a much lower price. The majority of the drugs in the market today are generic drugs. The generic drug manufacturer makes limited investments in research and development work; their focus, predominantly, is to manufacture in large quantities at the lowest possible cost maintaining the highest standards of quality. Most of the Indian pharmaceutical companies are in this category. Indian companies cater to the high demand for generic drugs in developed economies like the USA and Europe, taking advantage of the low manufacturing cost in the country. Unlike other industries, merely being a low-cost destination is not enough. The pharmaceutical industry requires a scientific environment, technical know-how, and commitment to quality. India has the advantage of a strong ecosystem of qualified scientists, the know-how of quality processes, and a network of supporting industries. That explains the leadership position India enjoys in the generic drugs space with pharmaceutical giants like Sun Pharma, Dr Reddy's Lab, Cipla, Lupin, etc.

Proprietary pharmaceutical companies also manufacture and market generic products. But, unlike proprietary drugs, on which only one manufacturer has the exclusivity to produce and market, generic drugs can be manufactured by any manufacturer. That means there is competition in the market for a drug with the same formula, and cost plays a big role. Over the years, Indian pharmaceutical companies have mastered the art of efficient manufacturing while maintaining high standards of quality. Though, initially, Indian pharmaceutical companies were the contract manufacturers for giants of the West, they have now built their own branded generics business, which gets them better margins.

The Indian government is aggressively supporting this industry with various schemes and policy support. Reducing dependency on China for Key Starting Materials (KSM) and Active Pharmaceutical Ingredients (API) is the primary focus. KSMs and APIs are raw materials without which a drug cannot be manufactured. Currently, India imports almost 35,000 crore rupees worth of API from China each year. In June 2021, the government announced a massive scheme with an outlay of 1,97,000 crore rupees to be utilised in 13 sectors, like Active Pharmaceutical Ingredients, pharma starting materials, drug intermediaries production, and production-linked incentives. The total outlay for bulk drugs is 6,940 crore rupees and pharmaceutical manufacturing is 15,000 crore rupees. The pharmaceutical industry remains core to the prime minister's push for an Atmanirbhar Bharat.

Of the sheer potential growth of this industry and the extensive economic impact, this is one of the industries Assam can focus on promoting. A pharmaceutical formulation manufacturing facility can have a huge impact on the economy of its host location. As the unit cannot fulfil all its requirements by itself, a lot of supporting industries get set up in the area. Industries for packing materials, printing, etc., are set up to deliver the required products to the unit. Large manufacturing facilities cannot fulfil all their manufacturing requirements themselves and are dependent on contract manufacturers to produce a part of their output. That's why a lot of small contract manufacturing units come up in the area. The success of the pharmaceutical industry in Hyderabad, Mumbai, and Ahmedabad gave rise to a lot of contract manufacturing companies, which helped boost the economy of the state significantly. The pharmaceutical industry provides fair compensation and a good standard of living to its employees. The employees with good disposable income help accelerate the local economy. Often a prosperous town is seen near a large pharmaceutical manufacturing facility.

As this industry is highly specialised, the right approach will be to attract established players to invest in the state. Incentives for a large pharmaceutical plant investment should go much beyond the standard subsidies. Sometimes, the offered subsidy may comprise a lion's share of the total capital investment. The infrastructure offered can be customised as much as possible in consultation with the prospective investor company. To get the right resources with specialised skills and experience to work in the unit, it should be located near a prominent city. Other incentives like transportation subsidies can also be provided.

With a lot of alternatives available, the campaign to convince pharmaceutical manufacturers for large investments in the state should be driven by the highest level of state leadership. The leaders should have one-on-one interaction with the heads of India's top pharmaceutical companies and present them with the advantages and benefits of investing in Assam. Pre-empting the requirements of the industry and addressing them while approaching a company for investment can be considered good salesmanship. There should be a willingness to accommodate the company's demands, and the government should be ready to provide a guarantee for uninterrupted business. But, what any profit-driven enterprise looks for is a fair return on their investment and long-term viability. The government should be proactive and be ready with the ROI model. It is important to note that the majority of the success of industrialised states like Andhra Pradesh and Gujarat is because of the entrepreneurial nature of the government and the salesmanship of the government representatives.

The pharmaceutical industry has changed the fortune of some states in India. Telangana and Gujarat are some examples whose economy is boosted significantly by the pharmaceutical industry. It is a tough industry to promote, but its contribution to inclusive prosperity can be matched only by only a few industries. Assam can transform its economy completely with its bet on pharmaceutical manufacturing.

Medical Devices

Many industry experts predict that the medical device industry will be one of the largest industries in the world. There are reasons to back such predictions. The demography of the world is changing. According to the United Nations, the global elderly population will increase from 607 million in 2015 to 1.8 billion in 2060. Covid-19 has also exposed the weak underbelly of medical facilities and services in various countries. There is an increased focus on enhancing medical facilities to address any such eventualities in the near future. There is also an increase in health insurance coverage for the population leading to high spending on healthcare. All these developments are pointing towards one fact. The medical device industry will expand manifold in the coming days, and for the states, this will be one of the key focus industries.

The industry is also going through a transformation. Historically, the medical device industry was dominated by global giants with large and expensive medical devices. In the last few years, there has been a movement to smaller patient-operable portable devices manufactured by small and mid-sized organisations. This is not only making these devices accessible but also making them affordable to a large population. However, there are still a majority of areas in which there is a prevalence of specialised medical devices. By and large, there is democratisation in the medical device industry and new disruptive players will define the success of this industry in the near future.

India's medical device market size was 11 billion dollars in 2020 and is expected to grow to 65 billion dollars by 2025. Currently, the Indian market is 75–80% dependent on imports. The government of India recognises the effect of this large import dependency on the overall trade deficit of the country and has announced multiple schemes to promote domestic manufacturing. The announcement of 100% Foreign Direct Investment (FDI) in the pharmaceutical sector to manufacture medical devices under automatic route is one of the significant decisions taken by the union government. In 2020, the government announced a Production-Linked Incentive (PLI) scheme with an outlay of ₹ 3,420 crore for the period of 2021–2028 for medical device manufacturing. The government has approved nine eligible projects by various manufacturers to manufacture medical devices with more than ₹ 700 crore investment. In the year 2020, the government set up a National Medical Device Promotion Council to promote the manufacturing of medical devices.

Various Indian states are also trying to grab the opportunity. Uttar Pradesh is setting up a medical tools and system manufacturing park in Noida. Punjab announced the setting up of a medical devices manufacturing park in Rajpura with an investment of 180 crore rupees. In January 2021, the Tamil Nadu government announced the setting up of a 350-acre medical devices park with an investment of around 430 crore rupees. The industry is also responding to the government's outreach. Companies like TransAsia Bio-Medical Ltd are setting up large manufacturing facilities in Telangana. A Japanese company, Omron also expressed large expansion plans in India. Indian companies are also not far behind. Starting from robotic surgical systems to wearable health monitoring systems, there are good innovative companies being set up across the country. The medical device industry is going through massive growth, and there is no better time to take advantage of this wave.

There can be a two-pronged strategy of developing a strong ecosystem of local entrepreneurs as well as getting investments from established players. The start-up policy can be specifically customised for the medical device industry to attract entrepreneurs to work in this area. For start-ups, devices for end consumers may be the focus area as it has less complexity than large equipment manufacturing. A state-of-the-art medical devices park that can house both large and mid-sized manufacturers is the need of the hour. The park needs to be a part of an industrial corridor in close proximity to Guwahati and should be well connected by road and air. It should be equipped with all the advanced amenities required for the industry. The government should put its efforts into building a strong start-up ecosystem for this sector.

To get the established medical device players to invest in the state, direct outreach is required. Medical device manufacturing is a capital-intensive industry with complex technologies. There are a lot of dependencies on external agencies for parts and sub-assemblies, some of which need to be sourced from outside India. The decision for investment needs to be backed up by a compelling business case. The government needs to build strong traction with Indian and global organisations. There should be a strong positioning strategy, the building of personal connections, the presentation of a cost-benefit analysis, and an aggressive campaign to persuade the companies with customised subsidies and incentives. The ability to customise the incentives will be critical as the motivation to invest differs from one company to another, and it is important to understand the key drivers and align the incentives accordingly. States like Gujarat and Maharashtra are regularly executing such tailored campaigns.

The medical device industry can trigger a larger play of high-tech manufacturing in Assam. If Assam can establish itself as a leader in this space, it can replicate the success of some of the established high-tech manufacturing countries of the world.

Iconic and Transformational Development

There are instances in history where transformational initiatives by various governments yielded massive results. There are examples like the building of the US interstate highway system around 70 years back, which brought economic prosperity to the nation. The Suez Canal development project is expected to bring massive development to the area in the form of industrial and logistic zones. Back home, the Golden Quadrilateral project undertaken by the A B Vajpayee government is considered to be one of the important catalysts for the country's industrial growth in subsequent years. Transformational development work in the area of information technology by the government of Andhra Pradesh in Hyderabad led to large-scale economic prosperity for the state. Even today, transformational projects like Bharat Mala and Sagar Mala are expected to make India an industrial powerhouse with inclusive growth.

Assam also can embark on an iconic project that will boost its economic growth significantly. One of the ideas for these centres around the most significant asset Assam possesses, the mighty Brahmaputra.

From time immemorial, rivers have been a source of Economic Growth of Nations. Apart from being a source of life's most essential element, rivers have been contributing as an efficient mode of transport, fulfilling the country's energy needs, and boosting the agrarian and marine economy. Take the example of the Yangtze River basin of China. This river basin contributes almost 50% of the country's GDP with 175 flourishing cities on its bank. Similarly, around 500 billion dollars of revenue and 1.5 million jobs in the American economy are generated by the Mississippi River basin. The Rhine is an economic lifeline of the industrial zones of Switzerland, Germany, and the Netherlands. Around 30% of Germany's coal, iron ore, and natural gas is transported along the river, where factories are set up to take deliveries for just-in-time manufacturing. The economy of Ukraine cannot be imagined without the Dnieper River. Three of the six largest Ukrainian cities are located on the bank of Dnieper, and it's the main mode of transportation connecting the inland with the black sea. The significance of the river can be clearly seen during the Russian invasion where the global food supply suffered massively because of the unavailability of this river route, and the cargo had to be shipped by railroad through Poland.

Assam has been blessed with a great river system with Brahmaputra being the lifeline for the social, economic, and cultural lives of Assam for ages. Historically, this mighty river was the main trade route to mainland India. The government of India recognises the importance of Brahmaputra as a strategic asset for industrial development and declared the riverway as National Waterway 2. Namami Brahmaputra was organised to create awareness about the gigantic economic potential of the river basin.

The entire stretch of the 890 km National Waterway from Sadiya to Dhubri can be developed as an economic corridor with a vision of industrial development on both banks.

The infrastructure development work required for this will lead to an immediate economic boost and the future economic prosperity of Assam. The development can be based on three core focus areas:

- Drenching and reclamation
- Ports and industrial parks development
- Development of river transport

Lowering the base of the river to ensure the movement of large vessels and strengthening the banks to stop any more horizontal expansion of the river is a critical step to initiate development activity. This will also resolve the issue of the yearly ritual of natural disasters. But, this has huge financial implications, and the cost outweighs the benefits significantly. The need of the hour is to link it to the larger goal of industrial development, build a profit-oriented business plan and market it to investors. Lands can be reclaimed and used to either build industrial areas or tourism infrastructure. The industrial areas can be developed on both banks of the river cluster-wise; each cluster will have an anchor industry supported by its ancillary ecosystem. For example, the automotive cluster will have an automotive manufacturing unit with the ancillary units located upstream. High-tech manufacturing and pharmaceutical formulation manufacturing, where there is a requirement for a large number of supporting industries can be other clusters to be planned. The quick and easy downstream river transportation from these ancillary units will ensure just-in-time delivery.

Major and minor ports can be developed keeping in mind the projected traffic and targeted turnaround time of the vessels. The development of feeder routes to the waterways can also be a part of the project. Along with the promotion of the manufacturing economy, another objective of this transformational program can also be tourism development. The small river islands can be developed as tourist parks with world-class amenities. River cruises can be promoted with a strong linkage to rural tourism. The beautification of the riverbank should be given immense importance. Needless to say, all these developments should be accompanied by energy generation and irrigation infrastructure. While the riverbanks can be the industrial hubs, the rest of the valley should get a massive boost in agriculture output from flood control and irrigation facilities.

To execute, the first step is to form a development corporation to conceive the vision, promote it to the stakeholders, transform it into an executable program, and manage it end-to-end. A master plan needs to be prepared dividing the large programs into multiple executable projects of industrial zones and tourism sectors. The business plans with return on investments and cost-benefit analysis for each of these projects are the next steps to follow. There must be sponsorship from the central government, but there can be a returns-based independent funding mechanism. Partnership with private enterprises to develop identified zones and sectors, setting up special purpose vehicles and joint ventures should be the order of the day. The generation of funds from the primary market and other government-guaranteed financial instruments can also be explored. Low-cost debts can be availed, provided they support the business plan and financial ratios.

The Brahmaputra Development Project can be a one-of-a-kind project in India with immense economic benefit to the nation. Once successful, this will be a model to replicate in other states with good riverine systems. This will be the perfect boost to the brand Assam and will be an ideal tribute to the prime minister's development initiative for the northeast.

Chapter 6

DRIVERS FOR INDUSTRIAL GROWTH

In pursuit of industrial development in the state, it is important to understand the drivers that will aid in the success of the endeavour. There are some states in India that are very strong in industrial growth while some others, despite having all the possible advantages have not progressed in the journey. Lack of consistent effort in some of the critical areas is the reason for this imbalance. Industrial development is led by private investments, and it is important to understand what drives private investors to invest in a state, why a business takes all the risks to set up in a particular location, and what are the ingredients for the industrialisation of a state. It is important to look at it from the perspective of an investor. What does a business or an investor look for in a state before deciding to set up their business there? Below are some of the factors.

Policy

The key driver for the industrial development of a state is an investor-friendly policy. There are many success stories of industry-friendly policies being responsible for the growth of an industry in a state. Karnataka and Hyderabad's IT policies and Gujarat's tourism policies are a few of them. It is not enough to just have a good policy; consistency of the policy is also important. Based on the type of industry, there are different ROI (Return on Investment) models and break-even structures. The investors add the financial benefit from the government policy in their calculation of returns. If the policies are not consistent and change frequently, the ROI is impacted. That's why investors always look for the stability factor in the track record of a state's industrial policy.

It is important to understand how the industrial policies need to be formulated. Firstly, a broad-based industrial policy addressing multiple industries doesn't work. It has to be specific to a type of industry the state intends to promote, sometimes specific to the extent of the type of products a unit manufactures. As an example, it is better to have a policy specific to a breakfast cereal manufacturer rather than covering it under a broad-based policy for the FMCG (Fast-Moving Consumer Goods) industry. This is very important for a state like Assam, which doesn't have the traditional advantage of an industrialised state. Unless a business doesn't see substantial and pinpointed benefit in setting up their business with a direct financial gain compared to other states, there won't be any investment. Industry-specific policies address the industry-specific nuances and help mitigate any potential risk.

This brings us to the point of the requirement of specialists in the industry department to help formulate the policy. There should be widespread deliberation with the industry before framing the state's industrial policy. These deliberations can be extended to the stakeholders of a few important potential investors. It is important to note that if the government can make the stakeholders of the target companies a participant in the process of formulation of the policy, it will be easier to attract those businesses to invest in the state later. This will also provide an assurance of the government's responsiveness to the needs of the industries. Such messaging is very important. There should be discussions with the CXOs and board members from the industry leaders to make them key participants in the process. Needless to say, this process requires outreach from the highest level of the government.

An industrial policy should cover some unconventional incentives, subsidies, and other benefits. It is important to understand that every state in India comes out with their industrial policy and the businesses will invest in Assam only if the return outweighs the potential risks to a great extent. There should be a fixed outlay for a period of time for a particular industry in the form of capital subsidy, working capital support, transportation subsidy, etc. Some innovative schemes to attract the experienced talents required for a type of industry will help the new industry to get the skillsets they would need. Right Production-Linked Incentives (PLI) for a specified period of time will make the industries gun for higher production numbers and, in the process, generate more revenue and employment. There should also be employment-linked incentives in the industrial policy.

In summary, industrial policy should be as granular as possible, formulated in consultation with the industry stakeholders and should have much more incentives than the other Indian states. The government will surely do the required cost-benefit analysis before rolling it out. But, a great policy is fundamental to a successful industrial journey for a state.

Infrastructure

Infrastructure is key to the industrial development of a state. A state cannot attract investment if it cannot boast of a world-class infrastructure for the smooth operation of the businesses. When talking about infrastructure, the first important element is quality road infrastructure. Placing the right products at the right time at the least possible cost is core to the success of an industry. Same way, sourcing the raw materials at the right time and transporting them to the production facilities at the least possible cost is very important for an industry to prosper. For both of these, the right road network and infrastructure is essential. The government should focus on building industrial corridors with world-class road infrastructure. A robust road network also creates a strong brand for the state and demonstrates the industry-friendly attitude of the state. Assam should identify the industrial areas and build a road network to support the industries in that area. Many Indian states achieved a competitive advantage by focusing on road infrastructure. Tamil Nadu is one example. Today, Tamil Nadu is one of the most industrialised states of India. The Highways and Minor Ports Department has a singular focus on developing state-of-the-art road networks across the state. Today, there are more than 2,000 km of multi-lane state highways connecting the industrial areas. This is apart from more than 2200 km of multi-lane national highways network. The road network connecting the industrial areas to the ports ensures a rapid movement of goods at the least possible cost. The industries will indeed be attracted to such infrastructure. A strong road network is the basic ingredient for a successful industrialised state.

India has taken some pathbreaking steps for infrastructure development as a part of its look-east policy with a key focus on connectivity to the ASEAN countries as a response to China's attempts to dominate the Indian Ocean region. These countries are India's natural allies with no political or economic disputes with India. The Indian government has taken up some large infrastructure development projects to connect India's northeast to southeast Asia. Participation in Asian Highway-1 has the vision to connect India to 32 South Asian countries.

The cost of transportation is a key consideration for an industry to be set up in a state. The cheapest form of transportation is through the waterways. Also, for an industry dependent on the import of raw materials or an industry focused on exports, the proximity to the nearest port forms a crucial part of decision-making to set up their manufacturing unit. There should be a great focus on the development of National Waterways-2 from Sadiya to Dhubri and make it a primary mode of goods transport across the state. India and Bangladesh activated the traditional riverine routes for transportation and, in 2018, decided to develop Jogighopa as a trans-shipment terminal for the movement of cargo. Assam is blessed with thousands of kilometres of navigable waterways that can form the core infrastructure for goods movement. The strengthening of riverine routes and connectivity to the Bay of Bengal will not only serve the trade interest of the country but will also be an effective counter to the trade hegemony of China. Assam should continue to take advantage of the initiative of the central government and build all the required infrastructure for robust industrial growth.

One of the basic requirements for the industrialisation of the state is an uninterrupted supply of electricity and water. There has been significant reform in the electricity sector in the last few years. With great effort, India has become a power-surplus country. There has been a huge focus on electrification and ensuring reliable supply in the last few years. Now, the state governments are investing their efforts in increasing the efficiency of last-mile electricity distribution.

The proposed new electricity bill is a landmark legislation in the history of power reforms in India in which the government is trying to distinguish between the infrastructure and distribution of electricity. This will have a direct impact on the service levels of the electricity supply. But, it is also important for the government to work on a plan to provide power to industries from renewable sources. It is important to have a vision of an industrial area to be self-reliant on electricity. The recent strides in both technology and the adoption of solar power are going to ensure that the power supply is decentralised, and uninterrupted power can be ensured to the industries with localised generation and distribution. Similarly, there should be a focus on the uninterrupted supply of water to the industrial units. Traditionally, Assam never focused on a robust water supply network as the majority of the state had an abundance of water from natural sources. However, industries cannot rely on natural sources as possible disruption of the source will have a massive negative impact on the functioning of the industry. The government should build a network to supply water to the industries.

The most important infrastructure the government needs to work on is building industrial parks. Assam has been building multiple industrial parks to promote different industries in the last few years. However, it is important to recognise that choosing the right location for these parks is as important as building them. Industries look for multiple aspects while setting up their units. Cost of operation, distance from the nearest supply location, raw material availability, and manpower availability are some of them. An industrial park at a location that isn't commensurate with the cost of running and is far away from the raw material sources, skilled manpower, and the market will be very difficult to operate. But, if it is located within a large city, the cost of operations will go up. That's why it is important to consider all these constraints and requirements before setting up the park. It is important to have close coordination with the industry while making such infrastructure decisions. The infrastructure inside the park also needs to be customised as per the requirements of the industry the park intends to host. The idea is to think like a businessman, understand the needs, and make the right plan to address them. Needless to say, the right infrastructure is the most important ingredient for the industrial development of a state. Only states with the right infrastructure have been successful in their industrial journey.

Skilled Manpower

Industries need the right resources to run, and the success of a state is largely dependent on the availability of skilled manpower to run the industries. There are instances of multiple industrialised states of India whose successes are attributed to the robust availability of skilled manpower for various sectors. Karnataka's success in both IT and manufacturing is attributed to the large number of Engineering graduates produced yearly in the state. Similarly, Telangana's success in the pharmaceutical industry can be attributed to the yearly availability large number of Pharmacy graduates. Some states also put a lot of effort into building a strong skilled workforce to serve the needs of the industries. The government of India recognised this reality and set up the skill development ministry in the year 2014. Ministry of Skill Development and Entrepreneurship through the National Skill Development Corporation targeted to skill 24 lakh youths with Pradhan Mantri Kaushal Vikas Yojana (PMKVY) 2015–16. Based on the learnings of the campaign, the scheme was revamped in 2016 and launched as Pradhan Mantri Kaushal Vikas Yojana (PMKVY) 2016–2020 with an outlay of 12,000 crore rupees to skill one crore people across the country in four years.

Though these schemes and policies are path-breaking, the success of the skill development program is dependent on grassroots-level implementation. While the states have been trying to take advantage and meet the target of skilling the youths, it is important to work towards getting a skilled workforce absorbed in the industries as soon as they are ready.

The first step for the skill-development program is to have a clear understanding of the demand-supply equation. For an aspirational state like Assam, the program should be embedded into the industrial vision and policy of the state. Based on the type of industry the state would like to promote and the assessment of the number and sizes of the industries expected, the plan for skill development should be devised. Only an industry-specific skill-development program aligned with the projected resource requirement for an industry can be successful. Otherwise, these will only be numbers with no visible impact on employment or industrial development. It is important to have one ministry for industries and skill development to unify the objectives of both ministries. The sector-wise industrial vision of the state should have a skill-development plan embedded in each sector separately. In the industrial policy document, there should be specific references to the required skills for a particular sector and the government's plan of action to develop those skills. Needless to say, this activity should be done with participation from the industry, preferably from the businesses that have shown interest in setting up their industries in the state. It is almost like consulting with potential investors on their requirements and taking steps to meet those.

Some government-initiated skill-development programs will require basic academic qualifications of the resources. There should be an increased focus on professional education. The number of professional institutes like Engineering institutions, Pharmacy colleges, etc., in Assam is very less compared to some of the highly industrialised states of India. It is important to increase this number. The number of yearly professional graduates or diploma pass-outs works as a catalyst for the industrial aspiration of a state.

There should be a timely review of the programs. There should be an assessment of the number of resources trained vs. employment. The skill development program's success is also measured by the target vs. actual compensation received by the resource. A skilled resource not receiving the right compensation for the role they are trained for requires a relook at the skill development program.

The programs should be amended or revamped based on the performance of the program. The Key Performance Indicators (KPIs) should be identified and measured in a timely fashion.

Conducive Environment

This is the most important aspect Assam needs to address in its pursuit of industrialisation. The story of the industrial vision of Assam is repeatedly blurred by the disruption caused by political movements and extremism since independence. Assam lost a lot of time since liberalisation in 1992 in dealing with these irritants and businesses never found it prudent to establish their presence in the state.

There is ruthless competition in the business world. Every player needs to compete with multiple competitors in the same market for their pie. Price plays a significant role in determining the market share of a business. With the price of raw materials remaining more or less the same for every player, the contest is on building operational efficiency. The manufacturer who can manufacture their goods at the lowest possible price and maintain the right standard of quality eventually emerges as a winner. Operational efficiency can only be achieved by maximising the utilisation of all the resources in possession. If there is a disruption in their regular business operation, however small the disruption is, the operational efficiency is affected. The cost of producing their goods goes up and the profit margin shrinks or the loss increases. The resultant impact on the market ensures they lose their competitive advantage.

For many businesses in India, investment in Assam has never been on their agenda. Rightly so, as there is no compelling reason for an industry to come to Assam. Even if Assam could balance its geographical disadvantage with some great investor-friendly policies, the potential disruptions of business operations with strikes, agitations, and extremist actions had a repelling effect on the industries. On top of it, the culture of collection of donations by an uncountable number of organisations made life difficult for those who took the risk to invest in Assam. When the businesses compare it with the industrial climate of some of the other Indian states like Gujarat or Maharashtra, it is an easy decision for them. Though there has been relative stability in the political space in Assam in the last few years with the elimination of most of the extremist organisations and containment of agitations, the perception built because of a long period of these disturbances still works as a dampener in the industrial investments in the state.

Assam needs to do a lot to address these apprehensions. First and foremost, there should be a business continuity guarantee for any businesses setting up their industry in an industrial park. The government should be the guarantor in protecting the businesses from any possible disruptions arising out of agitations or other political disturbances. There should be monetary compensation to the industries if the government is unable to meet the specific Service-Level Agreement (SLA). This will be a revolutionary step in attracting investment to the state. The government should back it up with proper legislation banning any agitation, strike, lockdown, etc., within a 5 km radius of the industrial parks. There should be provision for punitive action including recovery of the compensation to be paid by the government to the industries from the agitators. This may require public debate and discussions for the legislation to be enacted. Before that, the government also need to educate the people on the advantages of industrialisation and the harm caused by the agitations. The local population around the industrial park needs to be taken into confidence. Local committees should be set up to ensure the smooth functioning of the park. All these are required only for the first few years. Once, people see the effect of industrial development on their standard of living, these disruptions will be a thing of the past.

The culture of collection of donations is a known nuisance in Assam. To represent the diverse ethnic and regional aspirations of the people, so-called nationalist organisations crop up in every nook and corner of the state. Most of these organisations have only commercial interest in their mind, and the way they make money is through forced collection from the businesses. To avoid any confrontation, which may lead to business disruption, the businesses quietly pay up, but the dissonance remains. In a modern industrialised economy, these are prohibitive practices. The government should frame strict rules for the collection of donations. Donations can only be voluntary and should not be demanded. There should be a public medium through which the organisations can appeal for donations and anyone interested can pay to the designated bank accounts. Visiting the premises of an individual/business or calling to demand donations should be made a non-bailable criminal offence.

Understandably, in a democracy, these are strict measures. But, Assam should understand the reality and battle of perception it needs to fight to get much-needed investment to the state. Drastic situations require drastic measures. These measures are tough but necessary for the industrial journey of Assam.

Governance

A couple of years back, in my interaction with the MD of one of India's top pharmaceutical companies, I asked him what kind of government he wanted in the state where he had his business. He said, "Nothing much. I just want a government that will listen to me." By the word 'listen', he meant a government that is sensitive to the industry's needs, ready to accommodate any just demand from the industry and strives to make life easy for the businesses to operate in the state. It is important for the government to be responsive to the industry's needs. The problems faced by the industry should be heard and steps should be taken to ensure their smooth operations. For that regular interaction with the industry leaders by the highest level of the government is required. The feedback should be taken seriously, and execution should be swift. The successful industrial states demonstrated these traits on the path to their success.

Another widely used term in the pursuit of industrial development is 'ease of doing business'. The World Bank Publication, Doing Business 2020 provides ten areas of business regulations that are included in the ease of doing business score and ranking. These are starting a business, dealing with construction permits, getting electricity, registering property, getting credit, protecting minority investors, paying taxes, trading across borders, enforcing contracts, and resolving insolvency. Some of these parameters are the responsibility of the central government. The Indian government is making significant progress in its performance in some parameters like resolving insolvency, enforcing contracts, paying taxes, and protecting minority investors. But, a lot of critical parameters for ease of doing business are in the hands of the state governments. Currently, Assam is in the 'Apires' category based on the implementation of the Business Reform Action Plan (BRAP). Moving to the 'Top Achievers' category should be the primary focus area for the government.

The most important aspect of ease of doing business is how easily a business can be started. There have been propositions like 'single window clearance' for starting a business. But, barring a couple of states, no one has properly implemented this system. There are permissions/clearances/registrations required from various agencies like municipality/panchayat, labour department, environment department, PF department, ESI, sales tax, etc. With the clearances come separate inspections for each department. Multiple inspections bring corrupt practices. It is a painful experience for an entrepreneur to set up their industry.

The government department sitting on environment clearances was the reason for a huge adverse impact on the industrial development of the country in 2010–14. There are also hardships of land acquisition. The existing law on land acquisition is not favourable to the industries. Land acquisition has become unaffordable and is a dampener for setting up new projects. Businesses lose a lot of money if the clearances are delayed. They need to depend on external borrowings to fund their projects and end up paying huge amounts of money to the lenders as interest without any productive activity. This creates stress on the businesses and sometimes makes them unviable.

The government of Assam should be sensitive to this and put its efforts into ensuring a smooth experience for the investors to set up their businesses. Single window clearance should be nothing but 'single window clearance'. The government should set up a department under the industries ministry with a clear objective to provide this experience to entrepreneurs. This is the only go-to department for businesses. They will submit their application and all the documentation to this department, and it will be the responsibility of this department to get all the required clearances for the business. There should also be an effort to make the land acquisition a steady affair. This is a sensitive subject and unless the local population is taken into confidence with a clear communication on the benefit the industry is going to bring to them, there will always be bottlenecks. Assam has the disadvantage of not having large tracts of unfertile land like Gujarat and Andhra Pradesh. Couple this disadvantage with the pathological dislike propagated by some organisations against the industries, Assam will have a tough time acquiring land for setting up the industries. That's where out-of-the-box thinking is required. The government should make the landowners a part of the success of the industry being set up. Right incentives should be announced to attract them to offer their land. Local industrial development committees should be set up, and there should be healthy competition among the regions/districts on industrialisation. The benefits of industrialisation should be published periodically so that the local population understand the benefits of it.

The ranking in 'ease of doing business' is a great branding exercise for a state. A high rank ensures that the businesses will consider Assam as a part of their plan when they invest.

One of the common challenges a state with industrial aspiration faces is the inconsistency of their policy. This happens more in a state or country where the political forces are poles apart when it comes to ideology and vision. A secure and safe business environment is the expectation of every business. But, if the policy changes drastically with the change of government, there is an understandable concern. The ideal industrialised states always keep the fundamental policy intact while playing around with the tactics. One of the burning examples of this kind of inconsistency is India itself. While, in general, Indian governments have always been investment-friendly, foreign investors always raised doubts about the inconsistency of the Indian state when it comes to policy. Retrospective taxation enacted by one of the previous governments has been a piece of repressive action, which did a lot of harm to the perception of the investment climate in India. Similarly, rolling back, the projects approved by the previous governments have been in practice in a lot of Indian states.

This kind of policy inconsistency is unacceptable for any industry. Businesses normally don't invest for a short time. A manufacturing unit or an R&D centre is a long-term investment. If there is a change of policy with the change of government every five years, there won't be any investment.

The government should take all the possible measures to communicate to the industry that the validity of any policy is not dependent on the term of the government. Irrespective of the government, it will continue. To portray a unified face, the government should reach out to the opposition and make them a party to the fundamentals of the state's industrial vision. Making an opposition leader a key member while formulating the vision documents or assigning the responsibility of leading a legislative delegation to woo the industries to the state can be a couple of unconventional but important steps. That way the industry will be assured of the fact that the benefit they were promised by a particular government will be honoured even if there is a change in government. In Assam, this may not be very difficult to achieve. There is some kind of civilised cooperation across political parties in Assam when it comes to the larger interest of the state, and if desired, this can be achieved. Care should also be taken that any policy decision should not encroach into the ideological reservations of the opposition parties to such an extent that it becomes politically impossible to honour it when they come to power.

While focusing on the near-term objective of promoting industries, it is important for the government not to ignore the long-term strategic view of developing Assam as an industrial powerhouse of the future. A very systematic planning paradigm is required to avoid any haphazard activity that will yield some value in the near term but will have negative effects in future.

The setting up of industries should be in designated industrial areas with a great focus on the environment, impact on the ecosystem, and protection of local heritage and culture. There should be a good regulatory framework that, without infringing on the functioning of the industries, can take care of the larger interest of the state and society. It is important to note that industries don't dislike regulations as long they are just and transparent. Effective government policies are the hallmark of the success of a state.

To attract investment from industrial houses, the government should demonstrate great salesmanship. Assam needs to be much more aggressive in its sales efforts than other states. It also needs to fight the battle of negative perceptions built over a long period of political disturbances. Also, there is always limited private investments vis-a-vis the requirements and states have been competing to get a share of the pie.

There was this legendary case of Narendra Modi as Gujarat Chief Minister wooing Ratan Tata with a message of "Welcome to Gujarat" when the corporate giant decided to move their manufacturing plant out of West Bengal amid protests over land acquisition. Very recently, the case of Andhra Pradesh sending a private jet to pick up the Chairman of Kitex group, the largest private sector employer in Kerala to bring him to Andhra Pradesh has dominated the headlines. In return, Andhra Pradesh got a large investment from the group, which was primarily a diversion from its original investment plans in Kerala. The government of India has also utilised the services of the missions and consulates in various parts of the world to promote its 'Make in India' program and even went to the extent of fixing targets for getting investments. The prime minister himself visited various corporate houses to pitch for their investment in the country. There is no alternative to this kind of salesmanship in today's world. The story of Gujarat and Andhra Pradesh shows that it's highly effective.

Assam should build a strong investment promotion organisation under the Assam Industrial Development Corporation with the objective of getting industries to invest in the state. Targets should be assigned and reviewed. The team should approach the mission from multiple perspectives. While brand-building for Assam remains a key focus area, the primary objective of the group should be to conduct institutional sales campaigns among the corporate houses. The pitch for various industries should be properly designed; the cost-benefit analysis should be presented; the competitive advantage should be articulated, and a compelling case should be made for the target organisation to invest in the state. The "Assam house" in various states of the country should be strengthened with senior professionals to lead these campaigns. The chief minister himself should be the primary sponsor in this. He should review the progress of this team, give his suggestions, and strengthen the campaign with his personal connection to the Chairman and MDs of large corporations. There may be a requirement to take some exceptional steps to lure the investors, and the team should be empowered to take those.

There should be quid-pro-quo investments. Large government procurements should have an offset clause for a particular amount of investment. Sometimes, the government can set pre-conditions for procurement only against an investment. It is to be understood that investments don't flow automatically, they require innovative, consistent, and long-term efforts. There is no doubt that many of these activities are undertaken by the government today. But, it has to be more organised, structured, targeted, and measured.

Maintaining Competitiveness

For resilient growth, maintaining competitiveness is very critical. India@100 report suggests effective market competition and competitive firms as new policy priorities for policy action. According to the report:

"India needs to make strengthening **effective market competition** a more central element of its efforts to upgrade business environment conditions. Deeply distorted market structures across many sectors currently lead to poor outcomes, undoing the significant gains made in factor input conditions. Regulatory frameworks that are unfit for the purpose and legacy market structures reminiscent of different times are holding India back.

Effective enforcement of competition policy requires an alignment with the new realities of digital markets and the existing market structures in India. Active policies to encourage entry and enable the scaling of competitive new firms are important given the imbalance between large incumbents and their fragmented competition. Market regulation needs to be used as a tool to encourage value-based competition that encourages firms to compete on productivity. In markets with a strong role of government, robust governance, and incentive structures are needed to mimic market dynamics. Across these policies, astute reform management that recognises the existing political economy of India is critical.

India needs to adopt a comprehensive approach towards enabling the growth of **competitive firms**. Enabling the growth of competitive firms will require deploying a range of supply and demand-side policies, moving beyond current enterprise and industrial policies.

Infrastructure investments to build physical and digital connectivity are critical for firms to be able to access new markets. Regulatory reforms and improved effectiveness of the judicial system have to be pursued to enhance the ease of doing business. Access to capital has to be dramatically strengthened to enable investment and scaling. Market opening domestically (regulation) and internationally (trade policy) can create important new growth opportunities for companies as digitalisation reduces transaction costs of taping into distant markets."

These are effective broad frameworks based on which the policies need to be formulated. Building competitiveness requires a multi-pronged approach as focusing on one or a couple of variables will not get a sustainable outcome. As an example, focusing on the cost of capital, efficient sourcing or labour costs can bring about cost-competitiveness, but it is not sustainable as any other location can achieve better efficiency in these areas and take advantage. Hence, there should be an emphasis on multiple aspects like innovation, productivity, quality, and infrastructure. A broad-based innovation agenda in all the areas across products, branding, manufacturing, HR processes, etc., is required to build resilient businesses. Similarly, stressing productivity and quality will fetch both the required cost competitiveness and larger and consistent market access. Wherever possible, standardisation can be brought to achieve both productivity and quality objectives.

Environment

Care for the environment is currently the most important aspect of industrial development. The government should form a strong sustainability organisation whose responsibility will be to formulate the policies and norms and monitor their enforcement. While extreme care should be taken to ensure that these norms don't act as disruptors to the overall industrial environment, it is very important to ingrain sustainability into every aspect of business set-up in the state. The norms should be shared transparently, awareness programs should be organised, self-declarations should be encouraged and a proper reporting process should be in place. Assam's environmental policies and goals should be in complete alignment with the national goal of reaching net zero by 2070.

Companies are also becoming increasingly committed to climate goals. They are tracking the climate impact of all their activities and trying to be net zero as early as possible. This helps in building their brand and also secure business as institutional customers are showing their preference for vendors with clear sustainability goals. This will be a strong driver for industrial growth for the next few years.

Assam's natural advantages, the Indian government's sustained campaign for the development of the northeast and the execution of the Assam Development Model, can make the state an industrial powerhouse and a strong contributor to India's vision as a developed nation by 2047. Days of conflicts and disturbances are a thing of the past and strong economic growth in recent years is one of the key reasons for it. There is also a need to change the mindset. The history of exploitation of the poor by the business class has made the general population very suspicious of any industrialisation by the government. People need to be educated on the benefits of industrialisation with various campaigns. The government of Assam should go beyond the traditional role of facilitator and creator of a good investment climate. In the next chapter, we will discuss why the government should play a more active role and how it should do that.

Chapter 7

ROLE OF ASSAM GOVERNMENT IN INDUSTRIAL DEVELOPMENT

US President Ronald Reagan once famously said, "The government's view of the economy can be summed up in a few short phrases. If it moves, tax it. If it keeps moving, regulate it. If it stops moving, subsidise it."

There have been many diverse opinions on the role of governments in business. Some opinions are in favour of a complete hands-off policy. They believe that businesses should be allowed to flourish or parish based on their own strength. There is another school of thought, which believes that government should have a say in the businesses that were promoted with government incentives. They say when taxpayers' money is invested in promoting businesses, the government should have a bigger say in their state of affairs. Another opinion is that the government's role should be limited to that of a regulator and should not anyway be involved in the dynamics of an industry. But, there is a generic agreement that governments should play an active role in promoting industries. But, once it matures and market dynamics start determining business outcomes, it should step back and get involved only when there is a distressing situation or misconduct.

For a long period, post India's independence, the focus was on building large government-owned capital-intensive enterprises. For private enterprises, license-inspection raj dominated the industrial scene till the late eighties, which resulted in abysmal growth numbers now famously called the Hindu rate of growth. The government's role during that period was of someone who ran businesses themselves and enforced strict restrictions on the ones run by others. As a result, businesses plunged, and it took decades to undo the damage caused by this flawed policy. Some sectors are still struggling because of the regressive policies of those days. For a long phase post-liberalisation, the government's role was to drive investments by easing regulations, reducing duties, and creating an environment conducive to business. Suppressed for a long time, the industries got a new life which was reflected in the growth numbers in subsequent years. From the beginning of the millennium, a strong emphasis was given to infrastructure development, which contributed significantly to industrial growth. Governments have become very responsive with quick actions on policy as and when required.

The state governments have also become proactive in attracting investments. There is competition among the states to get investment from private enterprises and attractive incentives are rolled out for that. One can't forget the battle between Karnataka and erstwhile Andhra Pradesh to establish themselves as the IT capital of India. Even today, states compete very aggressively to get large investments. The famous competition among Maharashtra, Karnataka, and Gujarat to get Vedanta-Foxconn to invest in their states is one of the latest examples. It's another matter that the partnership between Vedanta and Foxconn didn't materialise subsequently. These contests are healthy and desirable in any democracy. Competitive federalism is one of the important aspects of a prosperous nation, and India is rightfully on that path. Unfortunately, this kind of competition is limited to only a few relatively prosperous states of the country. There are many reasons for that, and lack of intent may not always be one of them.

Many Indian states have disadvantages, which are both natural and acquired. Assam is fighting with some inherent disadvantages in its pursuit of developing industries in the state. The foremost disadvantage is the perception of a weak investment climate because of decades of political turmoil. Since independence, Assam has faced one crisis after another in the form of agitations, insurgencies, and ethnic strife. Though the situation has improved over the years, there are still threats of agitations and ethnic disturbances because of which investors are reluctant to bet on the state.

Another disadvantage is the lack of land resources. States like Gujarat and Andhra Pradesh have lakhs of hectares of barren land that can be converted to industrial infrastructure by providing the required amenities. Assam, being a fertile land for ages doesn't have this luxury, and the majority of the land resources are occupied. There are other issues of infrastructure, primarily lack of access to a port. For a smooth movement of goods, quicker and cost-effective access to the port is mandatory.

Assam, being a landlocked state doesn't have that advantage and successive governments didn't put any effort to develop the river navigation through Brahmaputra.

Lack of business mindset and industrial culture is another big disadvantage for Assam. There were past stories of exploitation by industries and businessmen. The businesses in Assam were run by a few privileged people, and the difference in the level of prosperity between them and indigenous Assamese people made the people look at any business activity with suspicion. As a result, there were widespread anti-business feelings among the masses, and there was no effort to correct the wrong perceptions. The benefits of industrialisation were never explained to the people, and industrial development was never a political issue in the state.

In the current circumstances, direct competition with the industrialised states will be very difficult. An investor will prefer Gujarat or Maharashtra with its cheap land, perfect industrial climate, and good infrastructure to a state like Assam any day. Hence, there is a need for a different approach. In the earlier chapters, we looked at the model in which there can be an emphasis on promoting and developing local entrepreneurship along with the established strategy of trying to attract investment from outside the state. This will require more active participation from the government. The government needs to go beyond devising policies and be an active participant in the industrialisation process.

Governments have a well-defined role in promoting businesses. These are limited to offering incentives, which are either production-linked or subsidies in power, water, logistics cost, capital, working capital, or providing space at a subsidised rate in industrial parks, etc. Things changed in the late nineties when state governments started pitching to the businesses aggressively following all the tricks of an enterprise sales campaign to convince the businesses to invest in their states. But, it didn't go beyond that. Though the governments have been trying to develop local entrepreneurship by providing financial support, there has been no large and sustained campaign to develop native businesses in their states. Assam needs to change that, and that requires a much more active role of the government. While there can be a consistent effort to attract investment from established players from outside the state, local entrepreneurship development can take Assam's industrial prosperity to new heights. We will try to explain the specific aspects where the government's role needs to be more proactive. But, before that, let us understand some of the important action areas essential for successful industrialisation.

Firstly, an **industry-sector-wise task force** needs to be formed with clear short- and long-term goals. This task force will be responsible for planning, execution, and operationalisation of industrial vision for the industry sectors the government wants to focus on. The task force will have the dual responsibility of building entrepreneurship and attracting investment. It will form the policies and take ownership of technology collaboration for the specific sector under it. Providing marketing assistance, developing a quality control framework, and enforcing it will be part of their responsibility. In summary, the task force will be like a business unit of an Organisation that will be responsible for the inception, growth, and efficient operation of the units in a particular industry sector.

Industries need **land and a reliable supply of water and electricity** to set up their businesses and the government can be very proactive in creating land pools for use of specific industries. Special economic zones and industrial parks are fundamental requirements, but the important aspect is to assess the feasibility of an industry sector before identifying and developing a location. To manage the paucity of government land, industrial parks on private land can be encouraged and incentivised. An uninterrupted supply of electricity and water is mandatory in today's industrial world. There can be a utility guarantee scheme that will assure an uninterrupted supply of these services, and there will be compensation in case of any failure.

There is no better competitive advantage for a state if it can **generate skilled resources** for the industries. India has seen many skill development initiatives in the past. What is required at the state level is to have a granular approach to skill development linking it to the planned capacity of the industries. There can be sector-wise forecasting of skilled resources and a system to match it with the repository of available resources. For any gap, a time-bound plan for the production of skilled resources can be in place. An approach of incentivising niche skills and maintaining a pool of resources always available for the industry will be key to success. Needless to say, skill development programs should produce resources that are industry-ready, and hence, these programs should be conducted in close coordination with the industries.

We discussed the significance of **policy support** for industrialisation in the earlier chapter. What is important is to devise sector-wise policies with clear linkage to the goals set for them. Every policy can be linked to a quantifiable outcome which will help assess its cost-benefit. The policies with maximum benefit should be continued and aggressively promoted.

Lastly, **salesmanship** is an integral part of a state's success in industrial development, one area in which Assam needs significant improvement. The success of Gujarat, Maharashtra, and Andhra Pradesh can be attributed to the amazing salesmanship of the people in their governments. Entrepreneurs look for eagerness, intent, and trustworthiness of the government when they plan for investment in a state. Ministers and top bureaucrats can have one-on-one engagements with the owners of top businesses. The Assam Houses in various states work just as liaison offices. It's time to strengthen these offices and use them to engage with industrialists of that state. This team can literally be the regional sales team of the state to attract industrial houses to invest in Assam. There can be enablement programs for officers and government employees responsible for industrial development on techniques of sales management.

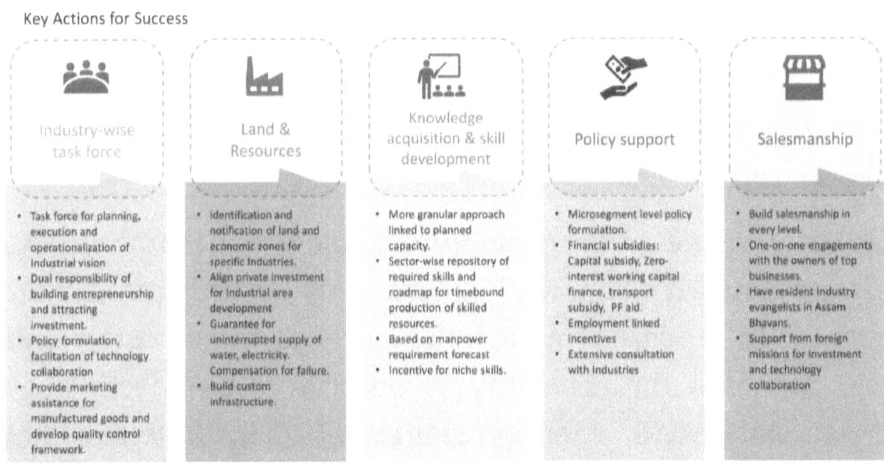

As discussed earlier, rather than competing with the other states, it is important for Assam to chart its own course of industrial development. For that, the role of the government needs to go beyond the traditional approach of announcing schemes and incentives. There must be active participation in building entrepreneurship and industries. Below are some of the areas where it can play an active role.

Academics and R&D

Every country that tried to develop industries focused on setting up world-class institutes for both engineering and R&D. Without a strong backbone of research and development, a resilient industrial environment is not possible. Assam can first focus on setting up state-of-the-art engineering colleges with curricula aligned with the requirements of the industries. There should be a good number of quality employable engineering resources churned out by engineering colleges, diplomas, and vocational institutes. Setting up R&D centres to address the specific needs of the industry sector is very important. These centres should focus on developing innovative products and solutions, highly efficient production systems, processes, new methodologies, etc., to aid the industries.

Technology Collaboration

The role of the government in technology collaboration was always muted. It facilitated, but never actively participated in the process. In the case of Assam, the newly promoted enterprises will not have the capability to build a case of technology collaboration with a foreign giant or R&D institute and that needs to be done by the government. A corporation under the government can act as an umbrella body to take ownership of the transferred technology. It can work on a strong business case for the utilisation of the technology by the enterprises it promotes, thereby, benefiting the owner of the technology.

Custom Infrastructure

Infrastructure development is by far the most important initiative by the governments to promote industries. Road, rail and waterways enable efficient transportation of goods thereby reducing cost and time to market. Industrial parks help industries to establish and grow their businesses quickly and easily. But, most of these infrastructures are generic in nature. Assam needs to go one step forward. Assam can build custom infrastructure specific to an industry. As an example, industrial parks for readymade garments can have floors designed to accommodate product lines with core manufacturing infrastructure like bus bars and centralised compressors. Similarly, meat manufacturing units must have designated production areas for different operations and should have integrated cold storage. Such custom infrastructure will ensure a shorter cycle from set up to output and help attract industries to establish their business in the state.

Ease of Doing Business

Ease of doing business is the most critical parameter to assess the investment potential of a state, and India, historically, is not a good performer in this area. If Assam needs to succeed, it should adopt a completely different approach for ease of doing business. For ease of starting a business, single window clearance is a much-talked-about phrase. The flaw in the current approach is that the onus of clearance lies with the businesses, and hence, despite the reduction of the number of agencies to approve a project, there are still struggles to get the clearances. Assam can shift the responsibility of clearance completely on the officers and make them accountable for the efficiency of the clearance process. It can go even one step further; the same agency can be given the responsibility to ensure a quicker operationalisation of the industry. All this can be managed online and monitored on a regular basis. For ease of doing business, there can be minimum physical government agency touchpoints, and the inspections can be conducted by third-party agencies. A well-documented process of standards and remedial action in case of violation should be published. An effective grievance redressal mechanism should also be put in place. Ease of doing business is most important for industrial development and government can make it a mission to improve it.

Promotion of the Industry and Produce

While the promotion of goods produced by the industry is the sole responsibility of the businesses, Assam will need to perform a more active role while promoting local enterprises and entrepreneurs. In the initial stages of the industrial development process, this will be far more important as the manufacturers and the goods produced in Assam will not be well-known to the buyers. The local entrepreneurs also will not have enough resources to approach the customers and develop the right strategies to market their products. A strong organisation under the government, which can help the enterprises market their produce, facilitate marketing tie-ups, and help execute clean transactions will be very beneficial.

Monitoring and Control

Continuous monitoring and building a control mechanism will be the key to success in Assam's industrialisation journey. The right systems and processes can be put in place for this. Key Performance Indicators (KPIs) and Key Result Areas (KRAs) should be clearly defined and monitored on a regular basis. A corrective mechanism can be put in place for any deviation. Information technology will have a very important role to play in this area.

Assam Industrial Development and Incubation Centre

To develop local enterprises, the government can form a corporation for industrial development and incubation of industries. The key objectives of this corporation will be as follows:

- Develop entrepreneurs through training and real-life business exposure.
- Develop executable business models and business plan templates for various investment brackets for focused industries
- Provide capital support
- Incubate businesses for a specific period of time
- Control marketing, quality, and financial discipline of the incubated enterprises
- Develop skilled resources to cater to the needs of the enterprises
- Build sustenance strategy for businesses after incubation
- Continuous improvement initiatives for building resilient enterprises

This centre can be divided into sector-wise COEs (Centres of Excellence) catering to each focussed industry. Each CoE will be a part of the industry-wide task force. The first job of the COEs will be to build business models and plans for various investment levels, which can be called 'model companies'. A model company is a repository of information and data points with the help of which a new enterprise can be set up and operationalised immediately. The details will be available at an industry micro-vertical level, e.g., a model company for readymade garment manufacturing with a 50 lakh rupees investment or a model company for a plastic bucket and ladder manufacturing company with a 10 lakh rupees investment. The core of the model company is a clearly defined business plan. As in any business plan, every aspect of the prospective business will be outlined with a clear financial projection, break-even, ROI analysis, etc. In addition to the business plan, there will be identification and listing of raw material sourcing options, potential customer options, and plant equipment and machinery souring details. A simulation of a business with all the manpower requirements and their sources will also be maintained. Using a model company document, a business can be set up at lightning speed with all the information available at the fingertips of prospective entrepreneurs. It is extremely critical to update the information on a regular basis to avoid any outdated and obsolete data. Model companies will be a unique but powerful tool for new entrepreneurs when they embark on their entrepreneurship journey.

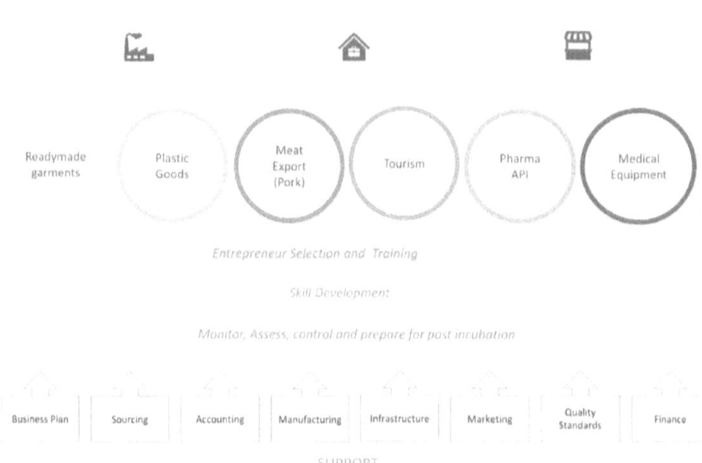

The important function of the centre is also to select prospective entrepreneurs from various parts of the state and provide them with training to prepare them for business. The selection process should be process-based and transparent to ensure that the right candidates are selected. Once selected, these candidates are provided with rigorous training for six months. The entrepreneurs selected from this program should be provided with capital support and incubated in the centre for three years. During these three years, there should be strict monitoring of the health of the business, and after the term, there should be an assessment of its readiness based on objective assessment criteria. If there is reasonable doubt of its ability to sustain itself as an independent entity, it can consider merging the business with other entities or be offered an exit route.

Skill development for the focussed industries is also a key function of the centre. Every year, the centre will work on a forecasting model to come out with the number of skilled resources required for each focussed industry based on which skill development program will run.

For the incubated businesses, the centre will monitor and manage a few aspects. The production and accounting processes will be monitored and a mechanism can be in place to keep both these disciplines on track. Quality and marketing are the two areas the centre will control directly. There will be quality control teams in each incubation centre that will be responsible for quality control of both raw materials and finished goods. Likewise, the marketing of goods will be supported by the centre. There will be a mechanism for the incubated companies to take control of all the functions by the third year to ensure they can sustain after the incubation period.

The centre will also devise strategies for sustenance for the businesses going out of incubation. Throughout the incubation period, it will monitor the health of the business with a rating system and intervene when the rating goes down.

Monetisation

Lastly, the government must have a plan to monetise any asset they build with taxpayer's money, and it should be a part of their overall plan. The government can retain a stake in the incubated companies, which can be divested at an appropriate time. In fact, the CoEs for incubation can be formed as separate entities that can have stakes in the companies they incubate. They can monetise it individually, company-wise, whenever appropriate or divest all the stakes in the portfolio companies once the sector matures and doesn't require any incubation support. Similarly, the model company information repository and knowledge base also can be monetised at the right time. Industrial parks or other infrastructure can also be potential candidates for divestment. There is no requirement to hold on to an asset once the necessity of government ownership is exhausted. The government's business is to promote industries, and for that, large funds need to be mobilised. It is impossible to fund everything with taxpayers' money, and there is a limitation of funding through debt. It is also an established fact that governments are not very efficient when it comes to maintaining assets, and hence, monetisation should be a key objective.

Though unconventional, these are implementable ideas. What the government will need is good intent and a strong team. Assam can demonstrate to the world how a proactive government can drive unprecedented industrial development in a state.

Chapter 8
SOCIAL DEVELOPMENT

The main objective of industrial development is to improve key economic indicators like GSDP (Gross State Domestic Product) and per capita income. But, these indicators are not sufficient to assess the prosperity of a state as they do not reflect wholistic and inclusive development. There can still be a lot of imbalance and disparity in the economic conditions of the people despite high GSDP and per capita numbers. Hence, growth will never be solid and resilient unless the benefits from it reach people from all social backgrounds and regions.

There are various measures used to assess a nation's progress in its human development goals. Human Development Index (HDI) published by the United Nations Development Program (UNDP) is one such measure of the wholistic well-being of a nation. HDI is an average of a country's achievements in three dimensions, which are: long and healthy life measured by life expectancy at birth, knowledge measured by expected and mean years of schooling, and standard of living measured by Gross

National Income (GNI) per capita in US dollars at purchasing power parity. While GNI is addressed through a focus on industrial development, the other two dimensions are also extremely important for the collective well-being of a nation.

No developed country can afford to have a low score on human development, which essentially signifies widespread inequality. Inequality is detrimental to resilient growth. Low performance in these areas comes in the way of developing employable resources affecting the overall competitiveness of the country. It also puts a huge stress on the government exchequer as the state needs to bear the cost in the form of health expenditure or sustenance support. It is also important to note that HDI may not be the ultimate index of measuring human prosperity. Some parameters like poverty and social inequality are kept outside its realm. On the measurement technique as well, a nation can score high with an intelligent combination of parameters without attaining overall prosperity. Despite all the criticism, HDI is globally accepted as the right measure for human development. There are other measures like the multi-dimensional poverty index that are used to assess poverty with 12-SDG (Sustainable Development Goals) aligned indicators. MPI is more relevant when it comes to measuring poverty beyond income.

India's rank has not been very high in HDI, hovering around 130 for the last many years. The same goes for Assam, which is ranked quite low in the HDI index among Indian states. Assam's problems have a lot to do with poor performance in specific geographies where archaic social norms prevail over any judicious consideration of child marriage and education.

Stunting remains a problem despite a lot of government initiatives in both the health management of expectant mothers and nutrition support to infants. These issues need urgent resolution.

Multi-dimensional Poverty Index (MPI) measures deprivations in the areas of nutrition, child and adolescent mortality, maternal health, years of schooling, school attendance, cooking fuel, sanitation, drinking water, electricity, housing, and assets and bank accounts. India has demonstrated marked improvements in MPI in recent years. According to the latest report from Niti Aayog, poor people, as defined by MPI, have reduced from 24.8% in 2015–16 to 14.9% in 2019–21. Assam has also shown phenomenal progress. Multi-dimensionally poor people in the state have come down from 32.65% in 2015–16 to 19.35% in 2019–21. Though there is commendable progress, these numbers need to come down further.

Enhancing employability in the labour market is another core objective in the area of social development. This is in alignment with the approach and effort of the government of India to have more people ready for employment. More than employment, the employability of the people is becoming a huge challenge. According to the World Economic Forum, only 25% of MBAs, 20% of engineers, and 10% of graduates are employable. In the larger labour market, there is a lot of skill gap because of which there is a lack of decent employment. The root cause of unemployment can be attributed a lot to unemployability than a lack of employment opportunities.

There are many reasons for these large skill gaps. Firstly, the current school curriculum equips kids with skills that are irrelevant in the market. There is a lack of emphasis on future skills. As vocational education is not provided with the same kind of importance as a degree, unemployable graduates are produced instead of ready manpower for the industry. There is a lack of collaboration with industries. The only interaction the students have with the industry is an occasional educational visit to a factory. Real-life experiences are missing and internships are provided close to the employment time. There is no early identification of interests, and no skill plan is devised for a student. The government is cognizant of these realities and trying to change the status quo. National Education Policy is one of the steps in that direction. In NEP, the government is trying to transform the way education and employability are connected. It tries to bring vocational training to mainstream education at an early stage in schools. Hands-on and skill-based education can be attained through deep industry-academia partnerships.

It is a fact that social development parameters improve with economic development. The theory is that with economic development, income increases and, with that, affordability for good medical facilities and education. However, the process of achieving economic prosperity itself becomes very difficult with a low level of human development. Governments have been working at the grassroots level in combination with various national and state-level programs in the areas of nourishment of children, access to health facilities for expectant mothers, incentivising parents to send their wards to school, implementing schemes like mid-day meals for nourishment and reducing drop-outs, etc. These are effective measures, but there is scope for more innovative action to achieve drastic improvement in this area. In the area of enhancing employability, the approach to skill development needs to be different. Interest identification and skill planning should start from early schooling at a broader level, which needs to be made more specific with higher grades. There cannot be an approach of one size fits all and a system-based approach is needed to align a student to a particular skill plan. Industry-ready engineering education needs to be provided to more students.

It is important to recognise that addressing such a complex problem with multiple variables requires superlative effort in a mission mode. It will take a few years to get the results of these efforts. But, it's still worth it. Without inclusive growth and better human development, the vision of a prosperous Assam will be a mirage. Though both the areas of social development and skilling look different in terms of their dynamics and prospective solutions, there can be an integrated approach to address these.

Let's break down each of these parameters and understand the possible approaches to address these. In the non-economic aspects of HDI, under the dimension of a long and healthy life, there are four indicators. Life expectancy at birth and neonatal, infant, and under-five mortality rate. It is well known that some of these indicators have their base set much before the event happens. The foundation of neonatal and infant mortality is set during the pre-teen years of the mother if not earlier. Hence, it is important to monitor and put a control mechanism in the entire lifecycle, from birth to the marriage of a girl, and monitor the required growth parameters for all children. Needless to say, this addresses the problem partially. There are other factors like access to better medical facilities that the government of Assam has been addressing proactively in the last few years.

Under the dimension of knowledge, there are three indicators. These are primary, upper-primary, and secondary dropout rates. Governments have been trying a combination of awareness creation and incentivisation to reduce these dropout rates. The first step to reduce the primary and upper-primary dropout to zero and secondary dropout to less than 10% is to take action as soon as drop-out happens. For that, firstly there is a need to have accurate information on drop-outs at the right time, and secondly, act swiftly to send the child back to school with various methods ranging from counselling to incentivising. There should also be preventive steps to avoid the situation, and for that, it is important to have information on the potential dropouts and take measures to stop them. This requires counselling and a feedback process powered by digital technologies involving artificial intelligence and machine learning. We will discuss this in detail in the later part of this chapter.

Enhancing employability in the labour market requires equipping human resources with the right industry-relevant skills. The first step of this is to understand the skills required and identify the ones that can be made a part of the vocational curriculum in the schools. Once identified, early interest should be discovered through formal and informal assessments and the students should be aligned to that skill with enough flexibility built-in to the plan. As mentioned earlier, industry collaboration is extremely important in each step of the process. There should be a clear path after schooling to be an expert in the skill through specialised technical education and exposure to industry.

A combination of administrative management and digital intervention can be a better way to move towards achieving the objectives. In the area of non-economic HDI, a central task force equipped with real-time information and adequate authority to direct any execution at the ground level is the first step. This task force can be structured district-wise and can further be divided into subdivisions and panchayats. This task force will track the progress and activities on the field and take corrective actions wherever required. There should be a fixing of accountability at all levels, and periodic performance appraisals should be conducted by the highest level of the government. Interdepartmental coordination is very important for the efficient operationalisation of the plan. Departments like social welfare, health, and education need to work very closely, and the task force at every level should have the right representation from each of these departments.

The skilling process should start with skill requirement forecasting and subject identification. Curriculum framing in coordination with the industries and developing skilling plans will be very important to build a structured program. Then comes the early interest identification and alignment of students at the school level. Industry assessments and internship programs should be an integral part of the program. A roadmap for each skill with multiple options for specialisation at a higher education level is extremely critical to building a sustainable path for the success of the program and the achievement of its final objectives.

Digital technologies can play a significant role in addressing the majority of these requirements. Right technology with analytical capability helps track every child and their progress in health parameters, school enrolment, dropout risk assessment, etc. Based on the insights from the data, a corrective plan of action can be put in place to contain any possible deviation. The entire system can be integrated from pregnancy to secondary education. The benefit of such an integrated system is immense. It can not only detect any health issues during the pregnancy stage that might potentially lead to the mortality of both the infant and mother but also identify any risk that could arise during a prospective mother's teen years based on poor health parameters. Remedial steps can be taken at an early stage to ensure any mortality risk that may occur in the later years. Also, the same system can be used to manage any potential dropouts by early detection of the indicators as well as early skill identification and alignment. A singular system can be envisioned to address the majority of the government's human development agenda. The technology platforms that are already in use should be revamped with new architecture and AI and ML should be included in their functionalities.

The digital platform should be able to record the pregnancy stages with details of the health parameters. The system should be able to flag any mismatch of health parameters to the relevant authority and corrective action will be recorded. Parameters for high-risk pregnancies will be defined, and all such pregnancies will be assigned to a special team to track and manage. The predictive engine will provide the potential cases of mortality that need to be brought to the notice of the higher authority in the government. Any number above the threshold needs to be immediately addressed with aggressive field action.

The same system should be used to record birth and each milestone of immunisation. The health parameters during birth should be recorded and rated. SOPs can be defined to manage children with low ratings during birth and an individual target-based growth plan should be worked upon. Any missing immunisation milestone should be alerted to the authorities for action. In the growing years, the BMI and growth of the child should be tracked in the system and a control mechanism should be in place in case of any discrepancy. Supplement delivery and consumption can also be tracked. Special health enhancement programs should be put in place for children with concerning health parameters and should be in place till the child is healthy enough to be moved out of the program.

The platform can be extended to the schools for tracking enrolment. Here again, any missing enrolment of a child attaining a particular age should be tracked and remedial action should be triggered. BMI and other health parameters should be recorded every six months to find out if there are any serious health risks. Malnourished children should be put under a special program and monitored more frequently. School attendance and performance recording should also be a part of the same platform. Based on multiple variables of attendance, socio-economic condition of the child, performance, health, etc., the system should have the ability to predict drop-out risk, and authorities can work closely with the school management to contain it. The objective and subjective data captured in the system can also be used to identify the early interest of a child.

This interest can be then translated into a detailed skill plan and executed in concurrence with the parents. A single system can be used to address the social development objectives of the government in the area of HDI and skilling as most of these Key Result Areas (KRAs) are interconnected and addressing one can have a strong impact on others.

The platform should be equipped with next-generation technologies like AI and ML. Artificial intelligence is mainly about understanding the world, learning, and coming out with decisions by replicating human experiences. Simply speaking, AI and ML can analyse massive volumes of data, understand patterns, make predictions, and help make decisions the same way human beings do. Using AI and ML, the system can analyse the patterns in the area of health and schooling and come out with predictions and recommendations. As an example, infant or maternal mortality or school dropouts can be predicted by the system by using algorithms. Similarly, recommendations for actions can be provided by a system that can be evaluated and executed. The integrity of data is extremely important in the functioning of such systems. Incomplete and inaccurate data affects the analysis of the impact, and the entire objective will fail. There should be data integrity checks at every level, and utmost care should be taken to maintain both the accuracy and totality of data. Biometric and video integration can be helpful in maintaining sanity. The system can be extended in future to many other areas like developing career growth plans for students, managing and improving academic standards, building a repository for future employment, etc.

A robust system-based approach with structured field-level execution can bring about drastic transformation in the area of social development. Talking about execution at the field level, building the right team with efficient people from the relevant departments as the task force is important. There should be clear time-based goals for each team and performance should be evaluated at regular intervals. There should be accountability at each level. Rewards and recognition should be announced for good performers and an environment of competition should be created among the teams. The achievements should be publicised widely to motivate the teams. The team should understand that this is a mission that may take years to finally accomplish, but baby steps can be taken and measured regularly.

Assam should take the giant leap to improve its Human Development Index score and increase opportunities for quality employment for its people. This is a significant milestone in its journey towards prosperity and will be a strong contribution to India's journey towards a developed nation by 2047.

Chapter 9

EFFICIENT GOVERNMENT ENTERPRISES

Inefficient enterprises put a lot of stress on the government's resources, which need to be utilised carefully to fuel growth. Inept service delivery from these enterprises also creates a bottleneck in the industrial aspiration of a state. Efficient government enterprises can be the perfect catalyst for economic growth and can help governments manage their finances better while focusing on service delivery. But, this is easier said than done. Worldwide, government enterprises are infamous for inefficiency, and it's a tough task to bring a change in the way these organisations operate.

Out of many reasons for the inefficiency of these enterprises, a few stand out prominently. Firstly, there is no strong vision that drives these enterprises. Most of them operate on a single-point mission of providing a type of service. There are routine monotonous activities that are performed by the employees without any concern about the outcome. For the employees, there is no lure of benefits or fear of consequences of bad performance. Most of these enterprises don't have the concept of rewards and recognition. The quality of their work will not determine their personal benefit, and hence, there is absolute insensitivity. The culture of customer service is missing as a lot of the enterprises are monopolies in their respective area; there is no fear of losing customers to competition and, hence, no effort to provide a better customer experience. The senior bureaucrats posted in the government enterprise consider their employment as a stop-gap arrangement before they get a more lucrative position in the government. Periodic performance assessment is also missing as most of these enterprises are very secretive about their operations. People come to know about their performance only at the time of the declaration of results. Lack of continuous public scrutiny makes them complacent and non-performers.

A common trait of non-performing government enterprises is that they are averse to anything new. New business models or processes are resisted aggressively. New technologies are never adopted, which takes the organisation on the path of rapid degradation. In the area of marketing, government enterprises are infamous for churning out the least effective marketing campaigns. Brand building always turns out to be a futile exercise in the face of poor customer experiences.

Lastly, enterprises are unable to get a fair price for the services they render. Any price increase is resisted very strongly by the common people making it extremely difficult for them to build a strong model for profitability. Governments put pressure on them to keep the price low and the enterprise further plunges into a deep black hole of inefficiency. The implications are clearly visible. As the government's focus is only on funding the losses incurred, the other important operating expenditures take a backseat. This explains the dismal state of assets held by these enterprises. With employee benefits and rewards taking the position far lower on the priority list, there is no focus on delivering good services and customer experiences. A vicious cycle of inept attitude leading to inefficiency that further leads to losses has been a familiar feature of government enterprises. These enterprises remain as white elephants, choking the government finances and blowing taxpayers' money.

Is it impossible to change the status quo and build efficient government enterprises? Not at all. These enterprises possess some of the greatest advantages, which private enterprises can only dream of. Firstly, most of these enterprises are monopolies in their respective fields. Having no competition in today's world itself takes the enterprise many steps ahead. There is the entire might of the government behind them. They can get the best terms from their suppliers as the trust in the government for monetary matters or adherence to agreed terms is very high. They can also attract the best of the talents as there is still a lot of affinity for government jobs. If provided with the right opportunities, enterprises can get the best human resources. Most importantly, with the overpowering impact of government in the day-to-day life of citizens, much less effort is required to build a brand. Even if the government enterprise faces competition in some areas, citizens prefer to take a government service if the quality improves.

Asian Development Bank made a few effective recommendations to improve the performance of state-owned enterprises (SOE). It says "To improve SOE performance, developing countries in Asia must ensure separation between the ownership and management functions of SOEs. Second, they must chart clear and quantifiable short and long-term goals, and appoint autonomous and competent management to strategise how to achieve these goals. Third, SOE management must institute transparent and independent monitoring and evaluation mechanisms to share regular performance reports of SOEs with all of their key shareholders and suggest improvements whenever needed. Finally, SOEs must attract qualified and talented people to join their ranks with competitive salary packages. These employees should be rewarded for better performance and penalised for chronic underperformance to establish a professionally competitive work culture to improve SOEs' efficiency and profitability."

In Amrit Kaal, the efficiency of government enterprises will contribute significantly to India's march towards becoming a developed country. For the last few years, there have been sustained efforts on the part of the government of India in this direction. Indian Railway is a perfect example. There has been a revolutionary improvement in service delivery. Be it cleanliness, on-time performance or world-class trains, India has seen marked improvement in rail transport in recent years. This proves the point that with the right vision and strong execution, a government enterprise can be transformed.

For Assam, too, making the government enterprises efficient is an important area of priority to drive economic growth.

Assam is in a better position to make this a reality considering the relatively smaller scale of operation of these enterprises. The need of the hour is to have a clear strategy and execution plan to rebuild these enterprises. We will discuss three government enterprises in this chapter and try to discuss the key areas of efficiency improvement. Some of the steps suggested may already have been initiated or put into action by the government.

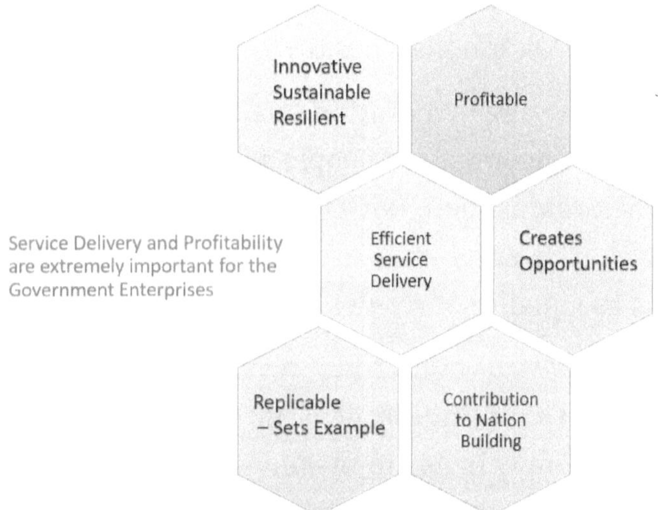

Assam State Transport Corporation

State Transport Corporation is one of the most important enterprises affecting the lives of its citizens daily. It is extremely difficult to run a profitable state transport corporation as there are welfare aspects involved in its operation. Assam State Transport Corporation faces the same kind of challenges as any other government enterprise. Under intense price scrutiny, the business fails to generate enough cash flows to run its operations and depends on the government to fund its losses. As scarce funds need to be used to just manage its day-to-day operations, the maintenance of assets is deprioritised. The quality of the assets deteriorates over a period of time until they are unfit for operation. With inoperative assets, the corporation can handle a lesser number of routes and the quality of service is affected. As a result, people move to private transport and alternate transportation modes. The revenue is further reduced because of that, and the corporation becomes unable to meet its day-to-day operational expenses. And, that's how a state-owned transport corporation marches towards its imminent death.

People managing corporations are often responsible for their degeneration. Incompetent people are given the responsibility to head the organisation. With the dismal state of affairs of the corporation, the employees are highly demotivated and that reflects in the quality of service.

Before any discussion on the revival and management of a state transport corporation, it is important to recognise that there won't be any change to the environment it operates. Price increases will always be resisted, and revenue generation will never be based on fundamental principles of business. Hence, innovative way of running the corporation needs to be explored.

Firstly, owning limited assets should be a core principle of the operation of the corporation. All transportation assets should be leased from private operators on mutually beneficial terms. The corporation can take the transport assets on short-term leases with the responsibility of managing booking and route planning. Other variable expenditures like salary, fuel, and maintenance can be the responsibility of the lessee. There will be a requirement to provide minimum guaranteed revenue to the lessee, which should be based on sound forecasting and route planning. ASTC already has a lot of private vehicles attached to it, but the need of the hour is to have a strong revenue stream out of it with an intelligent revenue model and contracting.

Secondly, as there will be price pressure on passenger transportation, alternate revenue routes should be explored. Intra-state cargo transportation is one such route. ASTC should use its passenger buses with spare capacity for transporting cargo and if needed use a dedicated fleet for cargo transportation.

Thirdly, the prime real estate held by the corporation can be the biggest money spinner for the corporation and potentially a big source of revenue. Long-term lease agreements can be worked out with large property developers to build commercial establishments and manage them. As these properties are in prime locations, they can fetch good revenue for the corporation. Also, the superior quality of maintenance can be expected as these will be managed by private enterprises. There is already some progress in that direction, but the process needs to be expedited. Here again, smart planning and execution are needed to handle the political implications of asset monetisation. There is also a need to generate cash flows from all land assets including the ones in remote locations that can only be handled through a consolidated contracting for a geography rather than monetising assets one by one.

Strategic outsourcing of some of the important services will be a very important step to make the corporation efficient. Ticketing and route planning can be outsourced to private parties with clear terms for price management and adherence to the targeted utilisation of assets to meet the minimum guarantee requirements. Maintenance standards should be set for the leased vehicles and periodic maintenance should be mandated in corporation-owned facilities. This maintenance service can be outsourced and can be another alternate source of revenue. The entire cargo operation can also be outsourced to experienced cargo operators with a revenue-sharing model. The corporation can act as a regulatory authority with clear guidelines for pricing, service, and asset quality and should run regular audits to control these.

So, the idea is to build an organisation where the corporation will own no assets and run no operations directly. What ASTC will own and manage will be its brand and promote it intelligently. The promotional campaign should have one single motto—creating ASTC as the most trusted transport service in the minds of the citizens. To achieve that, the ASTC team should take complete accountability for its operations and take ownership of all the KPIs. There should be a complete restructuring of the organisation and the human resources in line with the business model. There should be separate profit centres for each revenue stream of passenger transportation, cargo transportation, real-estate management, maintenance operations, etc. There should be revenue and profitability goals for each profit centre at all levels. In the districts, there should be a regional management organisation comprising each profit centre reporting to the regional head. The same structure will percolate down to the sub-division level. ASTC can define its own transport district and subdivisions based on the scale and complexity of operation that may be different from the established administrative units of the government of Assam. The generic services should be under the leadership of state and regional management. This matrix structure creates multiple points of accountability, and cumulative results, when amplified at the headquarters level, can be very high.

Caring for the environment should be an inherent belief system of a government-run enterprise. There should be an endeavour to switch to electric vehicles wherever possible. It is also financially viable as the operating cost of electric vehicles is very low and there are a lot of leasing options available from emerging players in the electric vehicle industry.

One of the most important areas of emphasis when it comes to running a successful organisation is the use of technology. ASTC should be an organisation powered by the latest technologies and the operations should be run on the right information systems. All the business processes like ticketing, fleet management, operations tracking, financial management, route planning, maintenance repair and overhaul, etc., should be technology-driven. The use of technology should be mandated for outsourced operations. A proper decision support system should be built with the help of AI and ML. Automation should be explored wherever feasible. The organisation always needs to be ready to face any disruption because of any new market reality or competition.

Lastly, the entire organisation should always remember that ASTC's primary responsibility is to serve the citizens of the state. Even if it achieves a larger share of the transport market with its revival strategies, it should never behave like a typical business entity with the sole objective of profit-making. It must keep citizen service as its core operating objective over anything else. The corporation should be kept away from political interference as much as possible. If the corporation turns profitable, there will be a lot of political interest that may not always be beneficial. A strong independent mechanism of selecting the head of the organisation and giving a fixed term can be the first step in that direction. At no point in time, there should be freebies for political personalities at the cost of the corporation's revenue and all appointments should be process-based and transparent. However, it is easier said than done.

Assam Power Distribution Company Limited

If one has to name the most stressed sector of government enterprise, it has to be the electricity distribution companies popularly known as the Discoms. The government-owned Discoms are highly inefficient, and they are regularly running into massive losses. The combined loss of this sector, in the year 2021, was around 90,000 crore rupees. These companies are unable to pay the generation companies for the power they procure, the overdue amount being around 67,000 crore rupees. This affects service delivery, and despite the availability of excess power in the grids, there are rampant power cuts. The aggregate technical and commercial losses, popularly called AT&C loss, which is basically loss in transmission, theft, billing, and payment and collection inefficiency is more than 15%. APDCL's situation has improved in the last few years with the government containing the losses significantly. Initiative on smart and prepaid meters is already increasing billing and collection efficiency and reducing leakages. There has been a lot of improvement in the ACS-ARR gap. In almost all other operations indicators, Assam's performance was good. On 31st March 2023, Assam was one of the top five states in Discoms quarterly performance rankings. Still, the AT&C loss is around 18%, and there is scope for improvement.

The use of digital technologies and automation can help bring the required efficiency in the Discoms. Using the right power forecasting tool will increase inefficiency in power purchase, supervisory control system like the SCADA system helps monitor distribution performance across the state. An advanced distribution management system comprising outage management and its integration into field force automation will ensure power availability. Integration with the GIS system helps track outages at the customer level. Similarly, automation at the last mile of power distribution helps balance the load on transformers; energy audit at all the levels of distribution helps identify and control transmission loss more effectively, and revamping the cabling infrastructure also helps contain the transmission loss. For commercial loss containment, the right ERP backbone with the billing system is very critical. This helps assess the collection performance and take any action in case of delays or defaults. A consumer app helps in improving collection efficiency and also getting much-needed feedback on the performance of the enterprise.

An important focus area for power distribution companies worldwide is to move to renewable sources of power to achieve the combined goals of decentralisation of power and sustainability goals. Though there are still challenges of generation and storage, renewable power is becoming more cost-effective than thermal. The cost of coal-based power is dependent on highly fluctuating coal prices and is costlier than renewable power. In India, private power distribution companies have made significant progress while the government Discoms are yet to catch up. Government Discoms should work on a strategy to implement more solar power projects both at the industrial and consumer levels.

Lastly, the Discoms should utilise the unparalleled strength of its reach to all the households in its area of operations and work on additional revenue models from it. In today's world, having a captive install base is the key objective of any mobile app. The Discoms get that advantage naturally. In the world of power distribution, where per unit price of power is always a sensitive topic, any additional source of revenue can provide the cushion required to run an efficient enterprise.

Assam Tourism Development Corporation

Assam Tourism Development Corporation (ATDC) is one of those government enterprises that has been doing some good work in recent years. There have been good efforts to build the brand of Assam and promote some unknown yet exotic destinations to the rest of India. The result can be seen in the increase in tourist footfalls. But, in a country like India where the entire economy of a state can potentially be run on revenue from tourists, the sky is the limit when it comes to developing tourism. ATDC has a huge role in the economic progress of the state and can be one of the best enterprises the government can boast of.

The sole objective of ATDC is to get more tourists to the state, both Indian and foreign. Indian tourists help get much-needed volume while foreign tourists help generate foreign exchange. The tastes of both these segments are different. While Indian tourists have the propensity to look for diverse tour experiences and would like to explore multiple destinations during their travel days, foreign tourists usually stick to a single unique destination, explore and experience it. The level of tourist infrastructure required by both these segments is also different. ATDC should have separate strategies to target both these segments.

For Indian tourists, a few circuits with a possible travel plan for a short trip (4–5 days), medium (7–8 days) and longer (8–12 days) trip should be identified. Once these circuits are identified, the possible itinerary and storyline around these circuits should be developed. This can be done in consultation with the tour operators and experts. Once, the basic work is done, the development requirements should be identified and executed. The existing tourist attractions in these circuits should be revamped and new experiences should be created. Every circuit should have an anchor attraction that works as a driver for the tourists. There should be a combination of natural and artificial experiences based on the theme. The accommodation capacity should be assessed and new infrastructure to be created if needed. At the end of the day, there should be a seamless story of a tourist starting from the entry point of a circuit and exiting it after a lot of experiences gathered over their tour period.

For foreign tourists, the key to getting their footfall is to identify the USP of a destination and build the brand around it. The starting point of this is to identify a target segment and build a positioning strategy. The theme and storyline should be in complete alignment with the strategy. Foreign tourists need quality facilities and advanced amenities for which there should be a clear plan of action.

ATDC should also try to work with private enterprises to build tourism infrastructure for business tourists for MICE (Meetings, Incentives, Conferences and Exhibitions). MICE constitute one of the largest chunks of value-based tourist activity. India has very few large convention centres with all the required amenities to organise global conferences. With its rise as a global economic powerhouse, it will need world-class convention centres like Hannover Messe of Germany or the National Exhibition and Convention Centre, Shanghai. It may sound ambitious, but the Indian economy is on an accelerator, and it will need large convention centres to support it. Assam has the perfect opportunity to be the first mover in this area.

Brand building and promotion is the most important part of any tourism development activity. In the last few years, Assam has also run some of the most successful campaigns to promote the state. But now it's time to move beyond that and promote specific destinations or tourist circuits based on its positioning strategy. There should be smart media planning to optimise cost and get maximum visibility. Tourism promotion is a collaborative exercise. ATDC should build a strong ecosystem of tour operations, bloggers, aggregators, online portals, etc.

The basic principle for government enterprises, as we discussed earlier in this chapter, should be that they should refrain from building and managing any infrastructure. Hence, it is extremely important to work closely with the private sector. This is a tricky exercise. The private sector will be interested only if there is business viability of a project and is backed by a strong cost-benefit analysis. A new tourist circuit may be considered to be highly risky for investment. It is the responsibility of the ATDC to build a strong business case to attract private investment. The first point is the business plan where a compelling case of the financial feasibility of a project should be articulated. Private Limited Enterprises or Special Purpose Vehicles (SPVs) can be formed with exclusive rights to developing and running the tourist infrastructure in a circuit or location. ATDC can also invest in it with a minority stake to provide the required confidence to the investors. There should be a clear exit strategy for the investors that will help mitigate the risk involved in the project. We discussed this in detail in one of the previous chapters.

Lastly, ATDC's role doesn't end with getting tourist footfalls to the state, it also has the larger responsibility to ensure pleasant and consistent experiences for tourists. While with the growth of the sector, the government of Assam can form special tourist police as conventional policing cannot cater to the unique nuances of tourism, ATDC can form support teams to help the tourists with the right information, address grievances and help them in case of any emergency. ATDC should also hold regular inspections and certify hotels and resorts based on their quality of service. It should also act as an enabler to build skills in tourism. It should facilitate training and skill development programs. In a tourist destination, there is always a possibility of conflict between the local population and the tourists. ATDC has the responsibility to not only address these conflicts immediately through the local tourist support teams but also should educate the local people on tourism and its advantages. It can be the biggest catalyst in the industrial development of the state in the face of immense opportunities in the tourism sector.

Well-run government enterprises reflect the efficiency of the government itself, which is very much required in a rapidly developing economy. The trust of people and businesses increases, which leads to increased investment activity in the state. Making government enterprises efficient is the best way to send a message to the world that "This government means business."

Chapter 10

INTELLIGENT GOVERNANCE

In today's world, there is no alternative to going digital, and it should be an integral part of running a government. Digital technologies make the government efficient without which the dream of a developed state will not be a reality.

Let us first understand the complexity of governance by virtue of the sheer scale of operation of the state. The government has to manage a state with a 78,438 sq. km area, around 3.5 crore population, 31 districts, more than 200 development blocks, 2000 *gaon panchayats* and 26,000 villages. The Finance Ministry needs to manage an economy of more than 5 lakh crore rupees and an expenditure of around 1.35 lakh crore rupees. Apart from all the governance issues in a complex state like Assam, the Department of the Home has to manage around 350 police stations with a budget of around 8000 crore rupees. The agriculture department has to manage around 30 lakh hectares of cultivable land and is responsible for more than 27 lakh farm families. The irrigation department is responsible for irrigation service on more than 5 lakh hectares of land. It has an added responsibility as only 17% of the cultivated land is irrigated. The fisheries department has the responsibility to enhance fish production from 2.86 lakh hectares of water resources and around 5,000 kilometres of river and tributary system. The PWD department has a larger network comprising highways and roads. These are statistics of only a few ministries. There are more than 60 prominent departments to manage and there are limited resources. In an environment where there is a need to manage large operations with a lot of constraints, the governance needs to be run intelligently and digital technologies play a larger role in that.

Governments cannot work in silos. There is the interdependency of multiple functions of the government to deliver effective governance. The Chief Minister and the key leaders of the state cannot rely on manually shared information, which is prone to errors and manipulation. In today's times, timely decisions based on accurate information are most crucial. With manual systems, the decision-making is delayed and often not based on facts. Governments cannot afford it, particularly when the state moves in a faster growth trajectory. The affairs of the state cannot be managed the same way it has been managed for the last 70 years. There should be a change in the way the information is gathered, disseminated, analysed and presented. The decision-making needs to be quick and based on real facts. The state leadership should be equipped with all the required information and system-based recommendations to make their decisions. There should be an explanation for every decision, and the root cause of any discrepancy should be explained. Next-generation technologies like AI and ML should aid decision-making rather than error-prone and motivated subjective reports from officials. The state needs to deliver intelligent governance with the help of digital technologies.

There are different stages of the adoption of digital technologies. It starts with the digitisation of records and departmental activities. There are many initiatives of the government to address this and as these processes are not very complex conceptually, this document will not delve deep into those.

The second level of going digital is implementing various applications for the effective functioning of government departments. These applications bring people, processes and technology together for the quick and efficient functioning of the government. The government of Assam has also implemented various such applications in the recent past. Below are a few examples of the applications that can provide the foundation for intelligent governance.

The PWD department can use a robust project management solution integrated with an intelligent road network monitoring system to monitor all the projects, costs, and health of the road network. Digital maps and satellite imagery can be used to monitor the health of the road networks, which helps in preparing yearly and quarterly plans to construct or repair the roads. Linking both these applications can also provide information on work in progress and the quality of work delivered by contractors. The 360-degree view of road infrastructure development can help the government to manage its projects efficiently and that is possible with the implementation of the right application.

The agriculture department can use a combination of surveillance, forecasting and analytics to measure the expected output and make important policy decisions pertaining to agricultural growth. The expected yield can be calculated in multiple ways starting from analysing the cropping pattern, historical analysis of yield, using aerial and satellite imagery to assess the cropping intensity, etc. Based on the analytics, the government can make decisions on procurement, welfare schemes, compensation to farmers, etc., based on real data. The decision-making is more accurate and faster.

Digitisation of health records and connecting all the government hospitals have been key discussion points for many governments. The health department needs to digitise all the records collected by the local health workers and hospitals for effective monitoring of citizens' health. These connected systems help keep a record of the health history of its citizens to provide more effective health services. The health department in turn gets the ability to assess the primary health risks among the population and take mitigating steps. The periodic analysis of the data will help the ministry formulate plans and policies pertaining to the health sector. We have seen in the earlier chapter how the health data collected by health workers can be used to minimise infant and maternal mortality.

The Finance Ministry can use strong financial forecasting tools to forecast the sector-wise growth and health of the economy and tweak policy decisions based on that. Real-time visibility of utilisation vs. budget is also important for future planning and any mid-year corrections. For that, the ministry needs to have strong analytical tools. The planning process can be completely digitised, and decentralised planning and control systems should be enabled. Data and Analytics should be made the core of governance and decisions should be driven purely on real-time facts. There can be dashboards for digital governance covering all the departments and the Chief Minister can use the same for fortnightly review of the ministries. Information backed up by grassroots data will help the government to plan and execute better.

There has been significant improvement in the functioning of government departments because of digitisation and the use of systems. The classic example is the way the state government's flagship scheme 'Mission Basundhara' was delivered. The program, which focussed on providing land rights to the landless and indigenous population and updating land records, could not have been executed without the aid of a digital platform. These operational systems are like a basic hygiene of governance and fundamental to the functioning of any citizen-centric department. There has been some commendable work in this direction, and it will accelerate in the next few years.

But, it is time to go beyond computerisation and discuss building a strong decision support system based on Data and Analytics. The government's approach to building a framework of intelligent governance can have four key focus areas.

Command Centre for Governance

The leadership of any organisation requires complete visibility of their operations. When it comes to a state, this visibility becomes extremely important. The leaders need to understand how the state is performing in every aspect of governance.

Running a state is very different from running a large enterprise. The complexity comes from the diverse business of the state and highly demanding stakeholders. The leadership's existence in their position is solely dependent on the five-year performance appraisal the stakeholders do. Balancing all these requires impeccable management skills backed by real-time information for decision-making. Hence, a central command centre for governance is extremely important.

Assam should have its command centre for government attached to the Chief Minister's office. This command centre will have the capability to monitor all departmental activities with required dashboards and analytics. It's a 24/7 live system with real-time updates of data from all the departments across the state.

The primary objective of the centre will be to provide complete transparency of the affairs of the state. Be it projects, welfare programs, health parameters, or law and order, the centre should be able to provide complete visibility to the state leadership. Let us understand an example of the user experience of the centre. The Chief Minister will be able to view the status of all the projects running across the state on a map depicting the project status graphically. The colour-coordinated view will immediately let the leader know the delayed projects, and they can drill down to see all the information related to that project like the location, details of the project, the contractor, responsible officials, the time and budget overruns, etc. He can immediately talk to the relevant officials to ask for an explanation of the delay, suggest corrective action, and note it for follow-ups. Similarly, he can monitor the status of the welfare programs in a dashboard in which the real-time status of the programs can be viewed. Here again, the CM and his ministers can assess the progress and suggest corrective steps in case of any deviation. In the area of law and order, too, real-time information on case registration vs. resolution, best and worst performing districts and police stations, the progress of citizen outreach programs, etc., can be monitored. Citizen's health parameters monitoring is another area that the command centre can provide visibility on. The real-time view of IMP, MMR, top diseases, doctor-patient ratio in a hospital, etc., can help the CM and his ministers take steps to improve the overall health situation in the state.

Another important aspect of this command centre is to build a Key Performance Indicator (KPI) based management framework that can be monitored regularly. Any performance-oriented organisation needs to assess, evaluate, and control its performance on the basis of some indicators, and the state is no different. The law-and-order situation in a police station can be assessed through the KPIs of filed vs. resolved cases, FIR to chargesheet time, report to response time, etc. Similarly, a sub-divisional office of the PWD can be evaluated with KPIs like on-time project delivery, project delivery within budget, construction quality, etc. KPI-based monitoring requires the initial step of identifying the KPIs and regularly updating them to ensure the right and executable KPIs are in force. The Chief Minister and his ministerial colleagues can review these KPIs in their periodic reviews with various departments.

The third important feature of this command centre will be the capability to address the issues emerging from the reviews. The command centre will be able to connect to any official over a video call to discuss any point related to their department's performance. There should be a provision to assign tasks to individuals and monitor the progress of the assigned work. One should be able to document the follow-up activities and report the progress. There should also be a provision for the participation of citizens from the remotest part of the state in the review and feedback process. One should be able to run complex simulations to assess the impact of any decision the state wants to take. We will discuss this more in detail in the Impact Analysis section of this chapter.

Needless to say, to build visibility through the command-and-control centre, the most important ingredient is data. The problem is not the existence of data, but the availability of it in the right form. It is important to look at the underlying systems to understand if the required data is collected properly and, if not, take measures to collect it. This is an evolving process, and a command centre formation need not wait till the completeness and consistency of data is ensured. It can start with a couple of departments with the availability of required data and roll it out to other departments later.

Predictive Insights

Can anyone predict the future? Well, the answer would have been a no till a few years back. But, with technology, it can be a reality now. With algorithms, there has been forecasting of market demand, weather, price, etc., for the last few years. Advancements in technologies like AI are making predictions even more efficient. The objective of this part of the chapter is not to discuss the systems and technology for building predictive insights. We will just take a few examples with the help of which the state can benefit from the adoption of predictive technologies.

One of the areas where governments, worldwide, are using technology for predictive insights is agriculture. Agriculture yield prediction can be extremely useful to understand the expected agro-output and determine any support to be provided to the farmers. This also helps assess the prospective state of the rural economy and formulate policies to ramp it up if needed. The state can also provide advisories to the farmers to cultivate a particular crop to maximise profit based on the prediction of the current crop mix.

Another area of predictive insights is utility consumption prediction. Based on causal factors like weather, festivals, industrial production, etc., utility consumption of the state can be predicted and the right sourcing and distribution decision can be taken.

Predictive insights can be used in the area of law and order also. There can be predictions on the increase of unlawful activities in a particular geography on the basis of which preventive steps can be taken. In the area of health, technology can be extremely useful to get predictive insights. IMR and MMR prediction can help the government focus more on specific regions to control the numbers. Disease prediction can be used to plan for specialist resources more efficiently. These predictions can help the government form effective policies.

There can be some ambitious plans to contain some high-impact complex issues with the help of predictive technology.

One of these areas is controlling the price of essential commodities. The government, with the help of the private sector and a combination of steps involving the use of technology and physical infrastructure, can target to make the state immune from large-scale price fluctuation of essential commodities. The near-impossible task of controlling the prices, which led to the toppling of governments in the past, can be a reality with predictive technology. The details can be discussed another time to avoid any deviation from the overall objective of this book.

Even here, data is the most important element. The accuracy of predictions is dependent on the extensiveness and integrity of data. While it is not possible to have all the accurate data from day one, there should be a start. Initially, the predictive insights can be used as one of the indicative inputs for decision-making before the predictions become more reliable and can be used for executive decisions and policy formulation.

Assam can be a role model in the country in adopting new-generation technologies. The benefit of these systems is immense and has the potential to transform the way governance is run in the country.

Low-Touch Governance

The essence of running low-touch governance is that the citizens should be able to get all their work done, problems resolved, and grievances addressed with the minimum possible number of visits to a government office. With the advancement of digital technologies, it is very much possible to achieve it. A perfect example of a similar transition can be seen in the banking industry. There was a time when it was unfathomable to do banking without a visit to a nearby branch. But, with the adoption of technology, consumers can get a complete banking experience without the requirement of visiting a branch at all. It is not difficult to provide similar experiences to the citizens with the right tools and policies.

Low-touch governance also plays an important role in eradicating the menace of corruption. A citizen's visit to an office raises the probability of bribes. Systems with the right monitoring, defined Service Level Agreements (SLAs) and an audit trail can help eliminate corruption to a great extent.

The first step towards low-touch governance is strengthening the citizen service apps. The government of Assam has also taken steps towards building apps to serve customers through it. There are two important success criteria for these apps. Firstly, it should be a one-point stop for a citizen to avail all the possible services of the government, and secondly, it should deliver a good experience for the citizens when they use it. The agenda for the government is to eliminate the visit of the citizen to a government office for services like paying a bill or applying for a service completely over a period of time.

The second step is to implement systems across the government departments where visits to an office can be avoided completely. As an example, the visit of a school office assistant to submit salary bills, reports, etc., can be eliminated by adopting online methods. The visit despite an online system should be handled with administrative mandates and the concerned official should be penalised. The visitors to a government office should be recorded and the reason for the visit needs to be explained by the head of the respective department.

The movement of files within the department should be monitored and any deviation from standard SLA should be flagged off.

Someone who is not equipped to handle these digital technologies should be provided with the facility of availing these through citizen service centres. Activities in these centres should be outsourced to private agencies with a track record of impeccable integrity, and there should be proper vigilance systems to detect any wrongdoing. The citizens should also be educated that the onus of completing their work is on the department, and there is no need to pay anyone for it.

A summary of the performance of these services should be available as a dashboard in the command-and-control centre, which can be reviewed by the administrative leadership of the state.

Impact Analysis

Like any other organisation, the government should also understand the possible impact of their decision. The traditional approach is to make a decision based on input from the field or research by professionals. Some of the decisions turn out to be highly effective and some are not. It is an endeavour of the government to make every decision effective enough to meet its objective. It's a difficult task, and impact analysis using digital technologies can help to a great extent.

The most effective way to analyse the possible impact of a decision is to simulate the scenarios. Private organisations use simulations on a regular basis before making their decisions. For them, it is not very difficult as most of the data required for this analysis and possible scenarios to be evaluated are available to them based on their past experience or inputs from external agencies on the business ecosystem. For governments, it's easier said than done. Hence, it's important to go step by step.

Here again, data plays an important role. Based on the implication of past decisions the system provides a perspective on the impact of any decision the government wants to take. While building such a large volume of data will be a continuous process, there should be a start.

There are massive possibilities for impact analysis the government can explore. Amazing insights may emerge from it and the government can use it to build effective policies and programs. For example, the government can assess the impact of its flagship "Arunudoi" scheme on some of the socio-economic parameters in society. There may be impacts on marriage and property registrations or enhanced women's hygiene. These impacts are recorded, and with data collected over many years, a trend can be established. It can be used for a more accurate prediction of the impacts of future welfare schemes. Digital technologies with available data points can establish co-relation between multiple variables and predict the possible impact of similar schemes based on the learning from earlier ones.

In every aspect of governance, impact analysis can help build a strong foundation for policy formulation. The impact of all the government schemes and programs can be analysed and reviewed. This can be extended to all the departments. There can be some impacts, which may be completely unconnected but can be explored. Based on the data collected, simulations can be run to understand what will be the future impact of the decision.

The impact analysis should be used as a powerful tool to evaluate the impact of a policy or scheme on the population. This can be an important pillar for running intelligent governance.

Command and Control Center for Governance

- ✓ Digital Cockpit for the Chief Minister and role-based interactive dashboard for other stakeholders
- ✓ Visualization of all the programs and projects
- ✓ Real-time view of progress of the government programs and schemes
- ✓ Monitoring of KPIs and performance Dashboards
- ✓ Smart collaboration
- ✓ Drill-down and Root cause analysis

Predictive Insights

- ✓ Predictive algorithm to gain future insights
- ✓ Based on historical trends and AI
- ✓ Examples: Agriculture yield prediction, price prediction of commodities, crime prediction, health prediction etc.

Low-touch Governance

- ✓ Strengthening citizen service apps
- ✓ Make departmental processes system based
- ✓ Citizen service centers to support digitally challenged
- ✓ Automation wherever possible
- ✓ Right control systems and SLAs

Impact Analysis

- ✓ Use of Big-data for impact analysis
- ✓ Impact of a variable on socio-economic parameters
- ✓ Examples: Impact of a cash transfer program on school enrolment, impact of a nutrition scheme on mortality rates, impact of agriculture scheme on yield etc.

One of the key principles of the current government is "Maximum governance, minimum government." The use of digital technology can truly help realise it. Assam can be one of the pioneers in the use of advanced digital technologies and can be a role model for other states.

Chapter 11

CONCLUSION

In this concluding chapter, we will discuss some of the critical success factors for building a prosperous state. These are extremely important action areas, which will determine the resilient progression of the state towards wholesome prosperity.

Elimination of Corruption

If we analyse the industrialised nations, there are a few common traits they exhibit barring a few exceptions. The first and most important characteristic is the near elimination of corruption from public life. No private enterprise can flourish in an environment of financial wrongdoing and investments diminishes in the countries where there is corruption. Countries like the USA, Singapore, Taiwan, Germany, etc., have very little corruption in public life. Countries like China have taken drastic measures to get rid of this menace by stringent measures. They have gone to the extent of jailing some of the senior-most members of the ruling party. Even countries like South Korea, where corruption was rampant a few years ago, took strong resolve to end this menace. They went to the extent of jailing the head of one of their most prestigious business houses, Samsung. There is a widespread recognition that industrialisation and corruption cannot go together. Not all these countries were clean when they embarked on their industrialisation journey but made it a point to take some drastic measures to handle it. Firstly, creating nationwide awareness and building perception among the people that corruption is an anti-national act, and anybody who indulges in it is a traitor. Both the bribe-givers and takers are castigated in the same way. The legislation on corruption is strengthened with exemplary punishments with the fast-tracked judicial process. And then, there is increased emphasis on systems and processes where personal engagement with the government official is eliminated wherever possible. We discussed low-touch governance in the last chapter. Implementation of technology systems and workflows in government functions not only helps reduce human contact that can put an end to any misconduct, but the inbuilt security and audit trail system can track any discrepancy in decision-making and analyse the root cause of any issue arising out of a decision later. These are fundamental action points for any government. There cannot be any tolerance for even the smallest act of corruption.

Respect for Free Enterprise

Another characteristic of successful industrial nations is their respect for free enterprise. By definition, a free enterprise is something where the government doesn't interfere in any aspect of its operations and markets determine its offerings and overall functioning. India to a large extent has managed to free the private enterprises from government interference barring a few strategic industries. This is commendable as the country has come out of license-permit Raj only around three decades back. But, it is also important to have respect for free enterprise among the citizens. For Assam, this is most important as in regular discourse, there is a visible disdain for businesses, particularly the large ones. There is typical resistance for large private enterprises, and it is perceived that industries and industrialists exist to exploit the poor. The commonly used word for the industrialist is "pujipati" in Assamese. The right meaning of the word is capitalist, and the very mention of this word creates a sense of hatred. This may be because of the history of exploitation of the common people by local landlords and tea-estate owners, generic depiction of businessmen as villains in various movies or a strong leftist movement, which made the people think ill about the businesses and the people running them. This needs to change.

People should be explained the benefits of capitalism. They should be made aware of the fact that people like Ambanis, Tatas and Birlas do a great service to the nation by paying crores of rupees of tax with which the welfare schemes are run. They provide employment to lakhs of people and help take a huge number of people out of poverty. The total corporate tax paid by the top 10 corporates in India is whopping 1.25 lakh crores. For the record, this is more than the entire fertiliser subsidy of the country. Income tax paid by the employees of these companies and the GST income from their products adds another few thousand crores to the exchequer. This is apart from the thousands of crores contributed by the private enterprises to various agencies as a part of their Corporate Social Responsibility (CSR) for the upliftment of the downtrodden and greater social good. People need to appreciate the role played by private enterprises in nation-building and respect them. Industries can flourish only in states where there is respect for them. People in industrialised states like Gujarat, Maharashtra, Tamil Nadu, etc., respect private enterprises immensely, and that's why there are very few stories of conflict. There is a need for a drastic change in the mindset of the people in Assam and the government with the help of the industry should take steps to educate the citizens.

Capacity Building in Administration

The prime minister mentioned the importance of building capacity in the administration many times in recent years. The topic is more important than the space it is getting in public discourse. The prime minister recognised the requirement of capacity building in administration long back and ensured that his personal administration included specialists and professionals. The same should be the case for Assam also. Generic administrative skills are not good enough anymore in today's world. Assam needs professionals with specialised expertise in a specific domain. One way is to have a robust enablement plan. Identification of skill needs, assessment of skill gaps and training people is a tried and tested way to build capacity. Another approach is to get professionals from other fields into the administration. This can be a highly effective way to build capacity provided there is enough attention given to change management. The government of India initiated the program of getting external professionals in a certain position in the bureaucracy, which was a limited success because of the inability to manage the assimilation of these resources in the established bureaucratic set-up. Much more thinking is required in this direction. But, capacity building in administration is important and key to success for a fast-growing economy.

Efficient Financial Management

When we talk about taking the nation on a fast trajectory of growth, efficient financial management by the government becomes extremely important. The government needs to invest heavily in infrastructure and other facilities and the dismal situation of the government's finances become an impediment to the growth story. The current situation is not great. The national fiscal deficit is around 6.4% currently. But, the combined fiscal deficit of the central and state governments is inching towards 10%. To get a perspective on how bad this number is, Sri Lanka, which is going through a massive economic crisis, is running a fiscal deficit of around 10.2%. There should be an immediate focus on improving it to avoid any economic disaster. Assam has been managing its fiscal deficit quite efficiently with a target of 3.7% in the fiscal 2023–24. This should continue. There should not be any wasteful expenditure or "Revdi" as termed by the prime minister. The revenue expenditure should not be funded by any debt. Instead, it should be used to build infrastructure and capacities. There should be tighter control on cost overruns in projects. Capital expenditure targets should be consistently met. Less fiscal deficit, high tax collection, high capital expenditure, and reduced revenue expenditure as a percentage of total spending will help the state on its path to prosperity. And yes, there should be strictly no "Revdi".

Concern for the Environment

There is one of the most critical global priorities of today, the reduction of carbon emissions. This objective coupled with controlling all forms of pollution is the foundation for governments and corporate's resolve to make this earth a better place. India has been quite aggressive in its carbon emission resolution. It is committed to its net-zero goal by 2070. This is highly ambitious for an economy with a rapid pace of growth. The businesses are also taking aggressive targets to reduce their carbon footprint and incorporating it as a part of their strategic plan. For Assam, having a resolute environmental protection strategy is far more critical than any other state.

The state has a very sensitive ecology with hills, forests, river networks and people who have traditionally amalgamated their lives with nature. Any development program should take into consideration this sensitivity and plans should be designed accordingly. A conflict may lead to disastrous consequences and will be very difficult to contain. The exploitation of nature for narrow commercial gain should be strictly prohibited. There should be unambiguous policies around the environment, and these should be enforced effectively. But there should be a perfect balance between the development goals and environmental protection objectives and there should not be any confrontation between them. India has seen stalled projects and economic slowdown owing to arrogant environmental activism by the governments in the past, and Assam should avoid that. Same with engagement with indigenous and tribal people. No state can prosper at the cost of its indigenous population. Assam is an amalgamation of people from hundreds of ethnicities with diverse backgrounds and cultures. The development efforts should respect these diversities and the unique make-up of society. These people should be an integral part of the development story. Any development effort excluding them will not be successful.

Containing Political Disturbances

The concluding chapter of this book will be incomplete without talking about the protests and agitations. We have mentioned it a couple of times in earlier chapters, but this needs re-emphasis. Assam has seen decades of instability with multiple agitations, extremist movements, and ethnic disturbances. The result of all these was underdevelopment. Till a few years back, there was almost no private investment and no new industries. The industries operating in the state were also forced to close down because of constant disruptions, extortions, and threats. Things have changed in the last few years. The people of Assam have realised that these agitations can only bring unending misery to the people while the agitators become wealthy. Those terrible days should never be allowed to come back, and the government should take even stricter steps to contain them. Protest is a right in a democracy, but if the protests and agitations take the state to a path of economic destruction, they should be summarily stopped. Agitation in Assam is becoming a profession for some people. They cannot be allowed to flourish at the cost of the entire population.

Focus on Education

And finally, an unwavering focus on quality education is the key to success for any state. It should be ensured that everyone gets an education, the right education, and quality education. The new education policy unveiled is a step in the right direction. There should be more attention towards quality education. Frequent updating of curriculum to match the changing global needs, continuous enablement of teachers and monitoring the health of education beyond the examinations will be essential in a growing economy. Education works as a strong foundation that can withstand any kind of tailwinds the state faces across its economy and socio-political aspects.

There is no other state in India with a better potential for industrial development than Assam. This may sound more like an emotional statement than a factual one. But, objective evaluation of the facts will also help support this. First, is the climate. Assam can boast of a climate that other states can envy. The lands are fertile, monsoon-adequate, water-abundant and have manageable pollution levels. There is literally no part of the state unconnected with a large water body. Both the Brahmaputra and Barak valleys have been expansively serviced by two large rivers. There is enough geographical diversity. There is no other state in India which is inherently plural than Assam. Completely diverse ethnicity can be seen throughout the state. These are some of the characteristics other countries try to develop in their pursuit of industrialisation. They are all present in Assam naturally. This century can very much belong to Assam.